DELHI

Delhi

The first city

edited by

MALVIKA SINGH

ACADEMIC FOUNDATION
NEW DELHI

www.academicfoundation.com

First published in 2011
by

ACADEMIC FOUNDATION
4772-73 / 23 Bharat Ram Road, (23 Ansari Road),
Darya Ganj, New Delhi - 110 002 (India).
Phones : 23245001 / 02 / 03 / 04.
Fax : +91-11-23245005.
E-mail : books@academicfoundation.com
www. academicfoundation.com

Cataloging in Publication Data--DK
  Courtesy: D.K. Agencies (P) Ltd. <docinfo@dkagencies.com>

Delhi : the first city / edited by Malvika Singh.
  p.   cm.
  ISBN 13: 9788171888887
  ISBN 10: 8171888887

  1. Delhi (India)--History. 2. Delhi (India)--Description and
travel. 3. Delhi (India)--Social life and customs.   I. Singh,
Malvika.

DDC 954.56   22

Typeset by Italics India, New Delhi.
Printed and bound in India.

For

AKHILESH MITHAL

Contents

Introduction

MALVIKA SINGH

The journal SEMINAR turned fifty in the year 2009. At that time we decided to bring out themed 'compendiums' from the vast treasure of material that the monthly had published over the five and more, decades. As part of that ongoing project, Academic Foundation have reproduced six special issues of SEMINAR, as a set of individual books, that celebrate the historic and famed cities of Delhi; Bombay, now Mumbai; Calcutta, now Kolkata; Madras, now Chennai; Hyderabad and Lucknow. We are delighted that this work will be accessible to a wider audience of Indians as well as visitors to India, who would want to share and experience the many special, personal and individual insights into the life and times of these cities, based on memories, on hitherto unspoken behind-the-scenes stories, some full of joy and others that lament the change, all of which are woven together in an extraordinary tapestry.

My gratitude to Rituraj and Sanu Kapila for having recognised the merit of these carefully crafted mini compendiums, and for reproducing them with much care. My thanks to all the writers who participated in the issues of SEMINAR, making them lively, unusual and substantive. To my colleagues at SEMINAR, my sincere thanks for supporting the many SEMINAR related 'ventures' like this one!

The first city

ANUPREETA DAS

IN the postcards they sell to tourists, the sky always looks too blue to be Delhi's. Perhaps the rectangle of untainted azure is meant to flatter the aesthetic sensibilities of the buyer, usually a sightseer searching for the prettiest picture to send home. But it could also be that the postcard maker decided to peddle, along with his photographic images of Delhi, a retelling of the city, where the sky's blue expanse isn't lacerated by the exhausts of 14 million people and their acquisitions and frustrations. He may have expressed his desire for a clean and uncluttered city through the symbolism of the clear sky.

Any retelling, after all, seeks to capture a bit of the ideal. And while constructing the ideal, whatever doesn't conform to the desired image is suppressed by the emphasis on what should be, or what used to be. Sometimes, the ideal is located in the imagination and sometimes, in memory.

Often, people who share a long and intimate relationship with Delhi refer to a past that was both ideal and idyllic. They talk gently of a time that was, letting memory sandpaper the rough edges of their experiences and film their eyes. As they dredge up the sounds, sights and smells of bygone days for a lachrymose rendition, the Delhi of the past – genteel, sedate and civil – becomes the ideal, or at least the better, city. Unstated in such a retelling is the wish to return to the 'better' past, or to recreate it wherever possible. While a far bigger historical past still permeates the city, it is the experiential past of a generation or two that has gone missing. It's what old Delhiites will talk about because it is the only past they personally know.

We're told of a city where trees lined the boulevards of Chandni Chowk, graffitied declarations of love and might hadn't yet defaced monuments and art and culture danced minuets in the living rooms of the gentility. There is mention of a New Delhi, young and proud, which Edward Lutyens would have recognized and revelled in. Delhi was the bureaucrat's city, well-mannered and peaceable, but also grand and powerful. As the capital of India, it continues to be the seat of political power and administrative control, but apart from this continuity, Delhi's past and present are divided by a chasm so wide and so disconsonant that memory could well be a construct of the imagination.

In the decades following independence, as New Delhi began to spread outwards slowly like a stain, the first of the fortune hunters and dreamcatchers trickled in from other parts of the country and outside, seeking power and opportunity. They tinged the city with a cosmopolitan sheen, but for the coterie that grew up in the privileged echelons of New Delhi, an idyllic home was being invaded. Old Delhi, too, was overrun by a new commerce that stamped out the unhurried way of life.

At this point, in any retelling that uses memory, the past has ascended to a pedestal and is ready to fall from grace into the cesspool of the present. Through what Delhi's older inhabitants call 'degeneration', the invaders, or the 'outsiders' pushed the city's past into the archives and installed a new rubric in its place. Under it, upward mobility was a direct function of money, entrepreneurial skills and proximity to power.

The newbies built houses and businesses wherever land was available. Some of them bought space in the nooks and crannies of refugee colonies. Often, they camped on the fringes of the city, and in due course, settlements sprouted and stretched the city's circumference. Colonies of workers emerged. These were people who partook of the amenities and facilities Delhi offered and made a grab for everything on display, yet refused to have a stake in city-building. For within their bedroom walls, they still thought of themselves as outsiders.

They grouped into nativities – Bengalis, Biharis, Bangladeshis, South Indians, Northeasterners, Kashmiri Pandits and Punjabis – or sought refuge in professional identities. They were Delhiites because geography and the pursuit of common goals made them so and not because the city offered a unifying identity. Delhi now belonged to everyone who lived in it, but no one belonged to Delhi. The original Delhiites too were missing from public life – they preferred the city of memory.

As the trickle swelled into a stream, every kind of migrant came to this city in search of work and play – the moneylender and his more contemporary version, the banker, the broker, the aesthete, the unskilled labourer, the refugee, the education pilgrim, the socialite, the fashionista, the politician from the hinterland.

They attached themselves, like bloodsucking fleas, to the arteries of power. At the points of rupture, ghettoes festered. Or they unthinkingly heaved their collective weight onto the network of infrastructure, pressing it down and breaking it up. The language they spoke was brash and fast-paced. Their ablutions choked the sewers and swelled the Yamuna. They swaggered into hotel lobbies, worshipped at the temples of commerce and lived in ornate houses. They built new schools and entertainment complexes.

Poorer migrants built their shanties around the new-rich colonies, and found work as construction labourers, bellboys, *chowkidars* and cleaners. A new social hierarchy based on wealth came to exist, and within each rank there were people who clawed their way through the city's fabric and claimed different shreds as their own. East and South Delhi, for instance, stood for very different classes of people. But each rank was linked by the relentless pursuit of Lakshmi.

When the sweat and dust and filth of their own trappings would not wash off their skins, the outsiders began cursing the city for its undelivered promises. They began to rue the lack of civic amenities and the paucity of water and electricity. They raged at the hair dryer blast of the sun and the ubiquity of dug-up roads. Even as they continued to suck the city dry, they moaned about the loss of faith in its provisions. Lured by the seemingly exceptional opportunities for wealth generation, creativity and entrepreneurship, they had flitted to Delhi like moths to a flame, but in the end it was their own hubris that had created the myth and was now shattering it.

Now they too have begun to reject the reality, searching instead, for an ideal. But unlike the older Delhiites, whose construct of the ideal city is supported by two frames of reference – the past and the present – the new Delhiites have no collective memory of the city. What they do have, from the jumble of frustration, dejection, impatience and intolerance that colours their interpretations of the city, are the ingredients for imagining an alternative Delhi.

In the imagination-based rhetoric of the new Delhiites, the ideal city, like the postcard maker's blue sky, is clean and uncluttered. Housing is orderly and adequate. Vehicular and industrial pollution does not suffocate the city's green lung. Neighbours are more than just familiar strangers while conversations between people are courteous. The Delhi Police is with you always. There is no shortfall of electricity and water. Streets are empty of garbage and begging children.

In the ideal city of the imagination, those with bureaucratic and political power do not misuse it for personal gains and transparency replaces games of intrigue. And in the final image of this slide show, the insecurity brought on by isolation – by people having to fend for themselves all the time – is effaced by the growth of a communitarian identity.

Perhaps there is already a sense, however inchoate, of what it means to be a Delhiite. The children of the outsiders have known no other city; for them, Delhi is home. They were born at a time when the process of disintegration had already begun, and they are growing up with the city's breakdown as a given, a matter of fact. The city's vastness, its contradictions, its buses and flyovers don't faze them. They are unimpressed by its status in the country, and dismissive of the festooning that happens on important days. After all, how awestruck can one be by home? Homogenized as they are by a post-liberalization culture of choice and a diet of satellite television, these children of settlers will eventually give the city its composite identity.

What that identity will be no one knows because the future, unlike the past, cannot be told. But the concept of the ideal Delhi, both imagined and remembered, can go a long way in shaping the future city. Retellings, therefore, are important. Not only do they keep a tradition of remembrance alive, but they also bequeath to the new generation cherished images of how a city should be.

The age that was

ANJOLIE ELA MENON

WHEN I write of the Delhi that I have known for half a century it will inevitably end up being a 'nostalgia piece', but I think this would be true if one were to reminisce about any major city in India today. Once beautiful cities have metamorphosed into unplanned urban jungles where almost everything new is ugly.

The first memories of my very early childhood are of Delhi Cantonment where my father was surgeon in the military hospital. Fifty-five years later, as with many cantonments, it remains the last bastion of calm, orderly cleanliness where old trees still stand, bugles sound in the distance and somewhat run-down but friendly bungalows bear testimony to an age that was. Everyone went around on bicycles and *tongas* were available for women to go to the market. Baird Place, where we lived, was set in a vast crescent of similar houses that have hardly changed over the years. In army houses what was important for us kids was the number of climbable trees in the compound. Here we had mango, jamun and three neem trees, a peepul and lots of *ber* and guava. A small tree house was built for us out of old crates where much of the household linen would mysteriously appear, not to speak of provisions from the pantry.

The cookhouse or *baborchikhana* was detached from the main house, but connected by a tiled roof passageway. There were three wood fired *chulas* with an oven underneath, a 'dooly' which was a wire netting fronted cupboard for keeping vegetables and also the cook's stash of *bidis* and a bottle containing the dregs of the *saab log's* whisky sodas!

A rickety wooden table was the only piece of furniture. Yet from this primitive kitchen amazing meals appeared. Not only delicious *desi* fare, but cakes and custards, pies and the flakiest pastry imaginable. For all the frugality of an army household where every bit of garden produce was used and processed into jams and pickles, one remembers a table always laden with marvellous food. Apart from occasional expeditions to Connaught Place and the rare treat – dinner at Moti Mahal – life in the cantonment was totally self-contained.

Years later in the mid '50s, when my mother died tragically, the family moved for a year from Baird Place to my aunt's house on 12, Willingdon Crescent. My uncle, Rashid Ali Baig, was then chief of protocol. The vast estate of Rashtrapati Bhavan was open to us to cycle about in and we swam in its wonderful swimming pool. This house, number 12, was later to be occupied by Mrs. Gandhi and it was while she lived here that Sanjay died and his body was laid out in the familiar central atrium.

It hardly occurred to us at the time that we were part of an extremely privileged set and we took for granted the vast acreage of lawns and gardens with their myriad birds and gorgeous flowering trees... gravel on the driveway, the faintly fishy smell of the untreated Jamuna *pani* that kept those lawns watered, the 17 servant quarters with *malis, dhobis, ayahs* and cooks on call, the *gwala*-on-the-spot who would bring a bucket of fresh milk to the kitchen in the morning... sleeping in the lawn in summer under mosquito nets, the smell of wet *khus* filling the house with cool sweetness... in the winter thick *rajais* and wood smoke, sitting on *charpois* peeling pine nuts on winter afternoons while grandmothers knitted and pickles ripened in the sun.

Ours was a family of inveterate picnickers and amateur archaeologists, so visits to all the famous monuments and some derelict ones were *de rigueur*. One could still climb to the top of the Qutub and we knew intimately all the tombs and ruins around it, including the eccentric 'Norman ruin', built by some homesick Englishman a couple of centuries ago. Our favourite spot for moonlight pictures was an abandoned Lodi period mansion called the Bistadari building. This lay within cycling distance in the *kikar* jungle on the other side of Kitchner Road (now Sardar Patel Marg).

We learnt to ride and it was possible in the '50s and '60s to trot down the tree-lined avenues of Akbar Road or Safdarjung Road. The Delhi Gymkhana Club became the favourite watering hole of our gang and one grew to know every book in that library. I was amazed to find some titles have not changed their position on those shelves for the last 50 years. Here, well-chaperoned girls would be subtly paraded on Sunday mornings while the band played and many a match would be made on the tennis courts. When Lutyens' Delhi was the only Delhi one knew, it seemed like paradise on earth.

The '50s marked an important watershed in the social history of Delhi. India was struggling to find a national identity and unlike Bombay, which was already cosmopolitan, the efforts of Delhi to find a style that suited the new compulsions of nationalism and post-independence pride were somewhat self-conscious. New institutions were being created and the norms for these were being laid down. These were the Nehru days and the beginning of the great era of Nehruvian diplomacy.

The Ashoka Hotel was built on a grand scale to accommodate the visiting delegations. Bulganin and Khrushchev, Queen Elizabeth and Tito, Chou En-lai and the Shah of Iran and many other important heads of state paid visits at this time. Panditji was extremely keen to 'Indianize' the type of hospitality to be offered. I remember my aunt Tara Ali Baig played a great role together with Indira Gandhi in deciding the new pattern for state banquets at Rashrapati Bhavan. Garlands replaced bouquets, Indian food was introduced, toasts drunk in orange juice in keeping with Gandhian mores, and bharatanatyam dancers entertained the guests after dinner. Several other modifications were devised to replace the old viceregal style, the best of which was that the ladies were not asked to withdraw after dessert!

There was a strange amalgam now of the austere values of a socialist republic and the remnants of the Raj typified by the grandeur of its monumental architecture and imposing ceremonies. In devising new rituals for the nation's ruling class the incongruities were abundant. A small anecdote to illustrate this is not amiss here. As surgeon to the president it was my father's duty to inspect the grounds and buildings of Rashtrapati Bhavan. Following his nose one day, to his utter astonishment he discovered six cows tethered to the gilded taps and fixtures of one of the grand bathrooms, steadily munching from the large marble bathtub. However, there was little he could do because he was informed that these constituted the First Lady's personal herd and that she liked to milk them herself.

Panditji and his young daughter Indira were closely watched by Delhiites in matters of style, both sartorial and otherwise. Fortunately for Delhi, and incidentally for India, there was a small band of dedicated women who took it upon themselves to preserve and develop handicrafts and the handloom industry, without any remuneration. Among them were Kamaladevi Chattopadhyaya, Shona Ray, Kitty Shivarao, Forrie Nehru and the indefatigable Prem Bery who ran the Cottage Industries Emporium for several decades. 'Cottage', as it was affectionately called, was not just a place to shop and hang out in, but became the arbiter of good taste and certainly dictated the lifestyle flavour of the times.

Chic women shed chiffon for Kanjeevarams, the young wore handloom saris, large *bindis* and Kolhapuri chappals. Homes were draped in handloom and tribal weaves, the floors covered in *chatai*, terracotta was all the rage and brass lamps replaced the chandeliers of yore. In those days the odious word 'ethnic' was never bandied about but a trend was definitely established which made it smart to be Indian. The *bandgala* replaced the three-piece suit and shocking pink and parrot green were no longer considered vulgar. Thus a distinct Delhi genre came to be which would ultimately ripple outwards.

After a brief sojourn in Bombay we returned to Delhi in the late '50s. We lived in 71, Lodi Estate which was eventually demolished and now houses the new INTACH building. My years at Miranda House marked yet another Delhi chapter in my life. The university was a world unto itself. The colleges and facilities were relatively spartan but the faculty was superb. Our interactions with St. Stephen's, which was in those days an all-male college, more than made up for the cloister-like atmosphere at Miranda House. We did several plays in collaboration with them. A sack-like version of the salwar kameez was in fashion but my friend Shama Zaidi and I got hauled up for appearing in college in pherans and churidars, the latter considered most unladylike. Pants were, of course, banned.

In those days, Hussain used to live in Naaz hotel in Jama Masjid and a group of us would often bunk classes to be taken to lunch at the Flora restaurant for a major pig-out. It is then that he organized my first exhibition in the garden of 71, Lodi Estate. Chandni Chowk was exactly half-way between home and university and my fascination for the culture of the bazaar that inspires my work even today had its genesis in my frequent walks through its *galis*. I knew my way around that whole area from Dariba to Khari Baoli, and often ended up in Paranthe Wali Gali to savour its splendours with a few like-minded friends. One had to ward off would-be eve teasers with an open safety pin. Predatory males, however, continue to be a part of the subculture of Delhi's streets.

Each passing era in Delhi has been witness to a changing set of players. In the early '60s the cultural life of Delhi was charmingly amateurish and somewhat dilettante. Charles Fabri, a Hungarian émigré and his brilliant Punjabi wife, Ratna, presided over the art scene. They both wrote on art and the whole milieu had the flavour of a saloon. Karl Khandelavala, Helen Chamanlal, the sisters of Amrita Shergill, Sir Malcom Macdonald, the British high commissioner, the dashing Count Ostorov and the French ambassador were among those who formed a small coterie of art lovers. Characters like Elizabeth Sass Brunner lent colour with her quaintly bohemian get up (usually a table cloth worn like a poncho). Roerich was much feted and talked about since he was Pandit Nehru's favourite artist and state patronage was important in those days. There was only Dhoomimal Gallery, which was part bookshop, and of course, Kumar Gallery, that young artists avoided because they were extremely rude to us. Aifacs, founded by the intrepid Bhabesh Sanyal, was the only venue for exhibitions and soon became a meeting ground for artists.

Satish Gujral lived in a barrack at Constitution House and my father took me reverently to meet him and his beautiful young wife Kiran. The Lalit Kala Akademi was in its infancy. The rising intellectual star of the time was art critic Richard Bartholomew, who ran *Thought* magazine, and as its secretary, steered LKA through those early years. People like Karl Khandelavala and Mulk Raj Anand lent dignity and stature to the institution which, unfortunately, fell into disgrace and obsolescence as the years passed.

I was married in 3, Akbar Road just after the '62 war broke out. There were restrictions on the number of guests so it turned out to be an austere affair with a tea reception the next day at the Rose Garden in Gymkhana Club. What was so different about the Delhi of those days was that there was no ostentation. 'Society' consisted mainly of bureaucrats, service officers, diplomats, a smattering of artists and writers and a few established families from Civil Lines in Old Delhi. There were no *nouveau riche* people; in fact almost everyone we knew tended to be *nouveau pauvre* instead. Even the politicians of that era shied away from public excess and practised a khadi culture. Delhi was yet to grow into a city and had the air of a genteel overgrown village.

After a gap of several years I returned to Delhi with husband and young kids in the late '60s. My father was now in a splendid house on Motilal Nehru Marg. Having been in a small flat in Bombay as a young naval wife, I savoured consciously, for the first time, the utter luxury of life in a Lutyens' bungalow. The splendour of our growing years seemed to be encapsulated in this brief sojourn. There was a small pavillion in the garden where we lunched in winter and dined by candlelight on summer nights. The sheer scale of that way of life allowed an open house and a constant flow of friends, lavish meals and conversation.

Indira Gandhi was now firmly in the saddle and Pupul Jayakar, as the 'czarina of culture', was setting new standards, very different from the amateurism of the '50s. By the early '70s, all the great new embassies had been built in Chanakyapuri. Vigyan Bhavan had become the venue for conferences and national events and the Republic Day parade, showcasing the new India, had become an institution.

Some colonies such as Sunder Nagar, Defence Colony, Nizamuddin, Golf Links and Friends Colony had begun to have a life of their own and Connaught Place ceased to be the centre of town. Meanwhile, the city was growing imperceptibly in a totally chaotic manner. Builder settlements developed in all directions swallowing up the old *lal dora* villages in their wake. A big land grab operation was on. With the land sharks at work, the Municipal Corporation was totally out of its depth and by the time the authorities began to wake up to the impending urban disaster, they were able to do too little much too late.

Where jackals had howled in the '60s, now hideous accretions mushroomed, devoid of proper roads, lighting or sanitation. Though the first flyovers were now being built to cope with the pressure on arterial roads, and the ring roads were built, it became evident that Chanakyapuri and Lutyens' Delhi were a separate city – still beautiful, well maintained and privileged – while out there beyond, citizens were expected to fend for themselves. So they created little walled and guarded ghettos and were responsible for their own security, hygiene and civic amenities. It was with dismay that we returned to Delhi in the mid '80s to find that the sedate bureaucratic city we knew, where the *babus* held sway, had become an unkempt, badly administered pseudo metropolis.

By the '90s, a loud and noisy population of nouveau riche puppies had taken over this other Delhi, flouting all those values that the Dilliwallahs had held dear. Worse still, this loudness and vulgarity began to impinge on 'establishment' Delhi as well, fed by the growing corruption and money culture that had begun to be all-pervasive.

Many five star hotels, eateries, restaurants, discos, boutiques, shopping malls and cineplexes had sprung up to cater to the needs of what have come to be known as the page three people and their wannabes. From the bleak days of only Doordarshan on TV, now more than 50 channels belt out the new pop culture. Weddings have established new and innovative levels of ostentation and vulgarity. The Delhi of today is rambunctious and clearly out to enjoy itself with its penchant for fast cars and constant entertainment.

However, among the many institutions that were created over the years, a few well-conceived and well-administered ones are worth mentioning. There is the Triveni Kala Sangam, founded and still run by Sundari Shridharani, for many years a haven for artists and intellectuals. Then, the India International Centre, which was wonderfully designed to endure by that great Delhi architect Joe Stein and ably presided over by Kapila Vatsyayan. The India Habitat Centre, which was perhaps Stein's farewell gift to Delhi. A beautiful example of monumental modern architecture, it is fast growing into an important hub for intellectual discourse and activity. In the wilderness of puppydom and the onslaught of McDonaldization, these institutions provide much needed oases of reason, restraint and excellence.

Today, politics continues to be at the heart of everything in Delhi. Soon, Lutyens' Delhi will be completely taken over by ex-prime ministers as one house after another gets converted into a memorial or is allotted to them or their heirs. Sadly, the Teen Murti House where Nehru lived was turned into a museum. These are symptoms of the immature sycophancy and lack of a sense of history that characterizes life in Delhi. This house should have been (like 10, Downing Street) the permanent residence of the prime minister of India. Perhaps one day it will be.

The turn of the century brought Delhi to the brink of disaster. The years of civic neglect and an ostrich-like refusal to acknowledge the mess resulted in burgeoning pollution, making the city a dangerous place to live in and one of the most polluted in the world. Many of the very rich had moved out to country mansions, euphemistically called 'farmhouses', in order to escape the pollution, but for the middle classes and the poor who live in the ever-expanding *jhuggis* and *jhopdis,* life became untenable. It was only in the 21st century that the government began to react but even now the remedial measures threaten to be overtaken by the still exploding population, even before they can take effect.

Yet we live in Delhi now, out of choice. Sometimes we wonder why. It seems to get hotter and dirtier each year, the traffic is impossible, people are rude and every Dilliwallah thinks he runs the country. In my studio in Nizamuddin West I work in the shadow of the great *dargah* of Nizamuddin Auliya, part of the continuum of the hoary history of this city. When I walk around Humayun's tomb at dawn, a dust storm gathers, bringing the smell of wet earth. A koel screams its brain fever song from a neem tree growing against ancient walls. This then, is where I want to be.

The hole under Delhi

PETER POPHAM

HUGE skies. Immense archaic swaying trees. The brain fever bird, the screeching parakeets, bird cries that seem more like the hooting of ghosts than any creature with feathers. Weather so big and heavy it sits on your shoulders like a doom. The long faraway bleating of the trains.

It's the most populated place I've ever lived in. I return to London and I can't get used to the silence, the emptiness. There's nobody on the street, or there is one person in navy blue dungarees and he's making an infernal noise with some machine. Hoovering up the refuse or trimming the hedge, he's just an adjunct to his machine, which, give a year or two, will manage without him altogether.

Delhi, by contrast, is thickly peopled everywhere. Everywhere the watchers, the idlers, the witnesses, the people whose only function in life (or so it seems) is to sit and watch with a steady, penetrating regard our comings and goings. Perhaps that is true of most places south of Marseilles or east of Istanbul. But what is different here is how the epic natural scale of Delhi dwarfs all of us – the drivers and sweepers and *chowkidars*, the ragtag army of loafing observers, and those like us who bustle in and out and back and forth on our important errands.

Nature in Delhi puts all of us in our place, which is right at the bottom of the enormous canvas, while Nature, Delhi's permanent imperialist, imposes its gigantic will. A vortex of wind sucks a ton of mushroom-coloured dust up from the gardens and streets and whirls it around, blackening the sun, then sprays it down on us. Or the trees thrash back and forth in the night, the windows slam and you come down in the morning to find everything thinly caked in dried mud. Or it's merely the sun, doing what it does in Delhi for more than half the year, scorching the sense out of us, roasting the sarcasm out of our pallid, northern souls.

The sun scorching down, the wind scouring the dust up from the plain, the rain clouds finally darkening the sky and performing that terrifying miracle of instant inundation... in any given season, in any epoch, the human element on Delhi's plain is ant-like, creeping perilously across the bottom of the frame. From Tughlaqabad to DLF, the scale of the plain and the elements that lord it here have goaded the human lordlings into hubris, into colossal gestures of domination. Why must Rajpath, Kingsway as was, be four times the length and twice the breadth of the Mall in London, the ceremonial avenue that culminates in Buckingham Palace? Because on the canvas of the north Indian plain, only gigantic will do, only the broadest, brashest strokes can dream of getting noticed, or of enduring.

From Tughlaqabad to DLF by way of Red Fort and Viceroy's House, they do get noticed, they endure for a season. Then the wind of history shifts and the futility that is always a lurking presence amid the pomp and grandeur, like the royal fool smirking in the shadow of the throne, jumps out centrestage and brings the house down, the fort down, the palace down, and the driving dust-heavy wind cuts through the ruined sashes and all that's left are lopsided mausoleums amid the thorny wastes.

What is amazing and tragicomic, what speaks volumes for man's indomitable vanity, is this: in the midst of such epic ruins, over and

over we start again, as if no such proof of the inevitable ultimate
destiny of what we are building existed – each time as if it was the
first time, brimming with hope and self-importance. Incapable of
conceiving the ultimate disaster as something that could, might, must
inevitably, happen also to us.

Other cities have this excuse: the follies and pompous pratfalls
of the past are buried hundreds of feet down, where silt and dust and
manure swallowed them up. In London, the deeper they dig the more
they uncover, going back to the markets and circuses of Londinium.
But in Delhi, the canvas of the plain is so huge, they could and did
build just anywhere. The ruins survive in all their splendid futility:
Hauz Khas, Purana Qila, the mausoleums of the Lodi kings. We live
among ruins. It's like living in a colossal graveyard; building the homes
that will become our own tombs.

Of course the process of deliquescence happens slowly, taking
far longer than the span of a single life, and because there are not (as
there are in London) particular plum spots which the city's masters
will always covet and build upon, because in Delhi you can start
afresh (lured by cheap land prices) just about anywhere, we see at
any moment three or four Delhis in different stages of emergence
and collapse. Shahjahanabad lurches into what one must suppose will
be its final phase of decline, the lanes and alleys clogged by traffic
and suffocated with fumes, the delicate *havelis* which enshrined the
old city's culture abandoned decades ago, the charm and refinement
almost impossible even to imagine any more? And Red Fort, the great
mother structure on which they all battened, a great sandstone cadaver
now, eviscerated post-Mutiny by the vengeful British, possessed now
by the termites of international tourism, who come away from it,
if they have any discernment, a little disappointed by its vacancy,
baffled by its enduring fame.

The new New Delhi, by contrast, is still hectically taking
shape, and is likely to be judged the least interesting of all the
Delhis that have come and gone. The high steel and glass towers at
its heart belong not to the north Indian plain nor even to Asia but

to our common commercial late 20th century civilization, which aspires to be the same whether taking root in Frankfurt or London's Docklands, in Seoul or Dallas or Gurgaon. But that is a superficial view: already the half-created new New Delhi has enough about it to make it very palpably a creation of these latitudes. The huge, enigmatic concentration of new temples at Chattarpur, for example, which will become perhaps as crucial to the latest Delhi as the Jama Masjid was to the one before last; the south Delhi 'farmhouses', as keenly realized an ideal of bourgeois living as a Lutyens' bungalow was an ideal miniature stately home for the servants of the Raj. And the roads that give access to them, the broad, tree-lined, beautifully cambered roads of Lutyens' Delhi, the rutted, pot-holed cart tracks that run past the farmhouses, each equally eloquent about the civic values embedded in both.

New New Delhi will come into its own; one can imagine in a few decades from now, when Race Course Road is deemed too vulnerable to terrorist rockets so that the PM must be moved somewhere safer, and when the President of the Republic clamours for a swimming pool and health centre in place of Rashtrapati Bhavan's Mughal Gardens, and when the first, second and third ring roads are all as clogged with cars as the lanes of Shahjahanabad are now? Then DLF will be the Delhi that people come to visit, while the works of Lutyens moulder among the thistles. They will come to stroll in the grounds of Sanskriti Kendra, to frolic at Fun 'n' Food Village, to say a midnight prayer among the crowds at Chattarpur?

But that will be then. What we have now is the Delhi of Sir Edwin and its outgrowths. This is our Delhi, where we work and play, live and die. What are its beauties, its absurdities, its lessons, its disasters?

At the core of New Delhi, in place of a beating heart, there is a question: why? It is a question that all the pageantry of 26th January cannot drown out, and the collected speeches delivered by successive prime ministers from the ramparts of Red Fort cannot fully answer.

The British decided some time prior to the Great Durbar of 1911 that Delhi should become the capital of British India in place of Calcutta, and the decision was announced by King-Emperor George V under the golden dome of the Royal Pavillion at the Durbar in December 1911. 'We are pleased to announce to Our People,' he gruffly declaimed, 'that... We have decided upon the transfer of the seat of the Government of India from Calcutta to the ancient capital of Delhi.'

Why was the decision taken? Was it merely to give some political point to all the flummery of the Durbar, to give George V something interesting to announce and the 100,000 invitees something to cheer? Was there some grand strategic purpose behind it? Or was it the action of an imperial regime increasingly embarrassed by its mercantile roots, increasingly anxious about the legitimacy of its rule, increasingly worried for the future?

The latter appears to be the correct explanation. If, as has been said, Britain gained her Indian empire in a fit of absent mindedness, 1857 was the wake-up call. Suddenly the entire imperial set-up was on the defensive. What was its purpose, its justification? Where was it headed? What was it all about? Questions like these, the merchants of Calcutta had been too busy minting money to ask, let alone answer. But as the steady clamour of newly educated Indians for self-government grew louder, answers had to be found. George V's pronouncement of 1911 was intended to be the last word on the subject: the British Raj was the legitimate successor to the last empire to lord it from Delhi, that of the Mughals. The inhabitants of India were 'Our People'. The King was India's Emperor. And the whole arrangement was to be rendered permanent by the creation of a vast new capital, to outdo in splendour all those that had gone before.

You did not have to be a bomb-throwing revolutionary back in 1911 to spot the shakiness of the arguments, the rhetorical sleight of hand that rendered the hundreds of millions of Indians 'Our People,' the underlying anxiety that persuaded the British to disavow their shopkeeper's smocks and claim instead the gorgeous robes of empire. Nor did you have to be a soothsayer to intuit that this grand imposture would not work, that it would not last. And of course, famously, it didn't.

The cement was barely dry on Viceroy's House before M.K. Gandhi was trotting up the steps for his first tête-à-tête with Lord Irwin. The British thought they were building New Delhi to embody their Indian empire for ages yet to come. Instead, they were fashioning a gigantic independence day present, complete with suitably awe-inspiring ceremonies, for the Congress.

It was, in retrospect, very kind of them. But there was a problem with it, and the problem has endured at least as well as the buildings. The problem has grown to maturity, just like the trees that border New Delhi's dreamlike boulevards.

New Delhi was an act of sleight of hand, an imperial imposture, the grandest of frauds. Merely changing hands, passing from white man to native, did not purge it of those qualities.

What is this fraud, this imposture?

When a parliament was built in Westminster, it was the culmination of many centuries of slow, erratic, experimental nation building. Parliament was the embodiment of centuries of trial and error, the strivings of many thousands of individuals to give political form to the nation's collective identity.

By imperial decree, New Delhi was called into existence as the capital of 'Our People' – in place of Calcutta, which could never be more than the headquarters of the merchants who built it. By an Act of British Parliament some 35 years later, it became the Dominion's, soon to be the Republic's, capital.

It was all too easy. Too magical. Too instantaneous. Smoke and mirrors, troops of gorgeously arrayed cavalry. Beating the retreat. Immense processions.

Ceremony stood in for substance, brassy declaration for gritty nation building. A ramshackle patchwork of unequal treaties, spanning the subcontinent, was somehow converted by the dazzling majesty of royal title into – 'Our People'. Then 35 years later, Our People became India.

Which is not to knock any of it: neither the architectural magnificence of Britain's new imperial capital, some of which has lasted very well, nor the slickness of the transfer, nor, God forbid, the World's Largest Democracy. I would only say: watch out. The superstructure gleams on top of Raisina Hill. But out of sight, obscured by decades of patriotic rhetoric, the foundations are beginning to look shaky. And the real India remains to be built.

A kayastha's view

RAVI DAYAL

SEMINAR'S letter seeking contributions to this issue on Delhi refers to 'Your city – where it is at, how it has changed and grown, and whether it has changed its identity.' Many solemn books on Delhi have been published over the years to confirm in stodgy detail what amateur eyewitnesses have long taken to be self-evident – that Delhi has, of course, changed enormously since the inauguration of New Delhi in 1931 and, more so, since 1947.

In 2001 the extravaganza of *The Millennium Book on New Delhi*, edited by B.P. Singh and Pavan K. Varma, OUP, was published. It deals with many of the issues now sought to be raised by Seminar and the bibliography of even that unscholarly volume lists some 80 titles. People have not only written on the monuments and history of medieval Delhi, but a great deal on the 20th century city, including its obsession with politics, and the fact that jackals could be heard on the outskirts of Barakhamba Road in the 1950s and *nilgai* roamed until later in the scrub now occupied by Pragati Maidan.

Many other details could be filled in to show how Delhi has changed: the expansion of the population from less than a million in 1946 to more than 12 million by 2000; the fact that you didn't need to boil or filter drinking water until the 1970s; could eat *kakri* and *chaat* from pavement vendors without falling terminally ill; could walk on grassy sidewalks in leather-soled shoes without damaging your heels and shins, as you would now on concrete pavements; could enjoy a boat ride on the Jaumna rather than be driven to attempting to do so in a fragment of the stinking moat below the Purana Qila, and so on.

Delhi is vast, and it is said to be a microcosm of India; it is inhabited liberally by people from all parts of the country and shared by all. Seminar's letter refers to 'Your city' – but apart possibly from the politicians who infest the city and have appropriated the prettiest real estate in it for themselves, do people still think of themselves as *Dilliwallahs*, as the Mathur Kayasthas of Delhi once did?

Born of Mathur parents, and having had an association with Delhi for as long as I can remember (i.e., from *circa* 1940), I have periodically thought of myself as an authentic Dilliwallah. Although much of my childhood was spent outside Delhi, we were annual winter migrants to the city over 16 years when I joined Delhi University and stewed for the next five (1954-59). Thereafter, I was based outside Delhi for the next 11 years as a student and then a publisher, and have been a publisher here since 1971. My genes, college days and profession have conspired to tie me to the city and coloured my view of it, so in this brief piece I will restrict myself to what flows from these three elements.

One of the traditional conceits of the Mathurs of Delhi is that they consider themselves the highest form of a high species – perhaps less flamboyant than the Mathurs once based in Lahore, but infinitely more refined as speakers of a tongue untainted by Punjabi; a cut above those in Rajasthan, who servilely served provincial rulers and said *hukum*; somewhat similar to members of the community in Agra and Lucknow, but free of the small-town smugness of urban U.P. The Mathurs of Delhi also considered themselves Dilliwallahs *par excellence*, forgetting that the city is now barely aware of them.

My father's family was originally from Peepalmandi in Agra, but with innumerable relations in Delhi; my mother's family was once based in Chelpuri and Chiraykhana in the Old City – always referred to as *shahar* by insiders, and never as Shahjahanabad. Early in the 20th century some Mathurs from these *mohallas* colonized spacious houses with large gardens in the Civil Lines area, mostly a swathe of land with *ber* orchards enclosed by Commissioner's Lane and Usmanpur (now Jaumna) Road. Many of them were lawyers, some became civil servants, others taught Urdu and Persian in colleges, and some concentrated on enjoying good food and music. Qudsia Bagh and the Jaumna across Bela (now Ring) Road were abiding factors in their lives – the river kept the area fragrant and comparatively cool, its sandy banks yielding walks and melons.

Some Mathur families were persuaded by the early developers of New Delhi to move to the new city. They clustered around Connaught Place, on Barakhamba and Curzon (now Kasturba Gandhi) Roads, and areas like Babur Road and Hanuman Road. All retained strong connections with their kin in 'Shahar' and the Civil Lines, and all the major shopping – whether for clothes, jewellery, spices, *paan*, tin boxes, books and stationery – was still done in the Old City.

You couldn't bypass Shahar. The entry into Delhi was always by train, at the Old Delhi railway station (the New Delhi station was largely ceremonial until the 1950s). There were usually prolonged unscheduled halts of the train at the Ghaziabad and Shahdara railway stations and, invariably, on the old iron bridge spanning the Jaumna, from where passengers had the classical view of the *dhobis* of Delhi washing and drying clothes on the river bank. The last phase of the journey was exhilarating as the train chugged through the Salimgarh fort and skirted the walls of the Lal Qila: the sense of entering a great and historic city was palpable.

The journey to a home in very central New Delhi was done in a *tonga* or two, with tin trunks and holdalls and baskets piled high. The route was well-trodden, the streets the tonga clattered through celebrated: it went past the Public (now Har Dayal) Library, down

Nai Sarak, then Chawri Bazar, past Qazi Hauz and on to Ajmeri Gate
(through which the tonga went, the horse's hooves echoing), past
Delhi (now Zakir Hussain) College and eventually down and up the
Minto Bridge slope (where the tonga moved at the pace of a pedestrian
and a gleaming Connaught Place came into view). Old Delhi was not
only an essential and hallowed part of the route, but also the place
where people indulged in sharp practices (with elegance), sharp talk
and, generally, were city-slickers in a city they ardently believed to be
the acme of creation.

As late as the 1950s the most trusted doctors in Delhi were
located in Chandni Chowk or Daryaganj, and the great tailor was
Mohammad Umar, who functioned in a lane not far from Atma
Ram's, the best bookshop in Delhi, and in the Kashmiri Gate area. You
didn't know good cuisine unless you had eaten in Shahar, and of the
four stylish hotels in Delhi, only the Imperial was in New Delhi: the
rest – the Cecil, the Swiss and Maidens – were in the Civil Lines area.
When a West Indies cricket team first toured India, it was housed at
Maidens, which rocked with calypso rhythms for the likes of Wallcot,
Weekes, Gomez and George Headley.

And yes, people went to Shahar to see and ride in trams, perhaps
the ricketiest, slowest and oldest trams in the world, but the only
ones in north India. Not even Lahore could boast of trams. Shahar
remained the heart and soul of Delhi throughout my days in Delhi
University. Our movements circumscribed by poor public transport
(perhaps the only element of continuity in Delhi), the lack of personal
scooters, motorcycles and cars, an outing from the campus usually led
to Kashmiri Gate or the Jama Masjid area: we often walked there, and
the route to Chandni Chowk meant using the high pedestrian bridge
across the railway track near Kash Gate and often emerging from that
exercise covered with soot from the puffing steam engines below as
they pulled wagons to or from the Old Delhi station.

Until the late 1950s even those living outside the city walls knew
Shahar reasonably well. New and Old Delhi together still formed a
comparatively compact unit, with New Delhiwallahs making regular

forays into Shahar and the Civil Lines areas: Moti Mahal was a premier attraction, and the bar and nightclub at Maidens' the fanciest in town. The Ring Road hadn't yet come into being, so people couldn't ignore the Old City.

The journey to the university meant rides through Daryaganj and past Lal Qila, frequently involving prolonged halts in these areas as buses were changed. During these halts one got to know the *dhabas* and stalls near the bus stands, and, if a suitable bus failed to turn up, the journey was often continued on foot or temporarily abandoned in the *galis* of the Old City. Commuters thus got to know the book-shops in Daryaganj and Nai Sarak, and the *kabariwallas* near the Jama Masjid. These meanderings also prevented some of us from forgetting the Urdu script entirely, for the hoardings and signboards in the Old City were still mostly in Urdu and it was reassuring to be able to decipher them.

The cohesive, urbane combine of New and Old Delhi no longer exists and while Delhi has grown into a vast city over the last few decades, its different parts don't seem to make up a whole. The area covered by it appears to have reverted to what it was before Shahar came into being – a collection of disconnected villages, each with its own ways and mannerisms, and altogether more provincial than the stylish, integrated city of not so long ago.

The village I inhabit, roughly extending from the Lodi Gardens to the Purana Qila, with Khan Market, several schools and Sujan Singh Park as its focal points, and the IIC, IHC, Humayun's Tomb, the Oberoi Hotel and Taj Mansingh at its periphery, is agreeable enough, but it's not a distinctive civilization, as Delhi once was. It is, nevertheless, a central area in a city that has expanded 30 kilometres afield in all the cardinal directions, and is visited by and known to people living in the outbanks. But most of the outbanks are less fortunate and remain strangers to each other.

There is, thus, no such thing as a Dilliwallah any more, and this absence seems to be part of the present, amorphous identity of the city. There are Londoners and New Yorkers, Parisians and

Mumbaikars, Mysoreans and Hyderabadis, but the inhabitants of Delhi are now anonymous. Even the Mathurs have stopped calling themselves Dilliwallahs. How can it be otherwise if you live in GK II, your spouse perhaps a Sikh, your son an investment banker in New York, your daughter-in-law an Italian and your grandson unable to digest a decent, spiced *kabab* made of goat meat?

While the Dilliwallah may have gone into oblivion, the other Kayastha conceit – of being traditionally literate and literary and, generally, good pen-pushers – has prospered in the changed environment. The Mathurs were quick to take to the new educational system introduced by the British and soon entered professions that needed the skills so acquired. Pedigree Mathur that I am, I became part of a comparatively new form of pen pushing in 1961 – publishing, and from my publishing peep-hole have not only witnessed and participated in the flowering of publishing in Delhi over the last few decades, but also been struck by the spectacular growth in Delhi's educational system and intellectual infrastructure which catalyzed publishing.

India's educational system is much derided, no doubt with good reason, but the good should not be interred with the bones: one of the good things is that in the hurly-burly of the last five decades, as Delhi shed its old scales and didn't quite refashion itself as a cohesive whole, it also became India's premier educational centre and a magnet for the country in this area. If Delhi has more automobiles than Mumbai, Kolkata and Chennai put together, it also probably has more authors than in these cities put together, and produces books in a similarly excessive proportion.

This wasn't always so. Until the mid-1960s Bombay was the major publishing centre in the country, with Calcutta and Madras not far behind. The best book printers and binders were in these cities, and even in 1971, when the OUP opened its office on Ansari Road, its bigger books were usually typeset there or in Pondicherry. With every major publishing house shifting base to Delhi around then or soon after, the skills needed to make a decent book rapidly developed in the region, and Delhi now leads the field both in printing and publishing.

Initially it was Ansari Road in Daryaganj that hosted the publishing renaissance, and manuscripts from Delhi University that nourished it, but matching the expansion of the city further south and the growth of author-yielding institutions in other parts of the city, publishing too is no longer concentrated along the rim of the Old City. Penguin are now in Panchsheel, OUP on Jaisingh Road, IndiaInk in New Rajendra Nagar, Permanent Black in Patparganj and Ravi Dayal in a back-room facing a garden and a pomegranate tree in Sujan Singh Park.

While the Delhi I knew and sometimes felt I belonged to has been obliterated, its new and, in many ways, much nastier incarnation has nevertheless nourished me enormously with the ideas its contemporary scholars, thinkers and writers have generated. A live but violent and corrupt Delhi is not a pleasurable creature to endure, but for a publisher in India, 'If on earth there is a place of bliss/It is this, it is this, it is this' crazy city.

The art of living

ARPANA CAUR

THIS is not the Delhi I grew up in. That Delhi was quiet and innocent, with very few cars, no television, many trees, and a routine rhythm of school or work, and leisurely walks on wide car-less streets.

When I began to exhibit in 1974, there were two galleries, two collectors, and two lines for the happenings in the art world in a couple of newspapers. One was considered lucky if even one person walked into a gallery. Friends would tease me: 'So, when are you having your next one-person show,' which meant one audience a day. So in 1981, I did my sad and funny 'Missing Audience' series with empty chairs but the singer singing alone in ecstasy, eyes closed. You somehow had to keep the flame burning.

It has become the past so soon, like black and white films.

Today's Delhi is multicoloured, it's the cultural capital of the country – a tag once attached to Bombay – with over a hundred galleries and an opening every day. As I write, for instance, there are openings of two senior non-Delhi artists, a discussion on women artists in a gallery in Defence Colony I have never been to, and a sculptor's performance at our own Academy of Fine Arts and Literature – all in one evening!

After a long day of painting, it needs courage to attend all these. One is usually selective but on a day like this, it is impossible to remain in one's shell much as one may love to.

This is Delhi. It will never allow you your cosy shell anymore !

Once upon a time contemporary artists from Delhi, Calcutta and South India simply had to go to Bombay to earn their bread, not butter, where the Sabavalas, Godrejs, Dubashs, Pundoles and Gandhys would welcome them with open arms. Long gruelling journeys, carting large paintings and their frames under train berths, staying at hard-to-get YWCAs, stretching canvasses overnight at the never-available Jehangir Gallery! Mumbai's was the open cosmopolitan culture, welcoming new forms of art. And Delhi, the staid *babu*-city that went to sleep at seven, earning the label of dull, boring and most of all, uncultured, an extension of the 'agricultured' North.

Today, the butter is all in Delhi. Galleries are always calling and cajoling artists, rather than the other way around. Not a day goes by without an 'interested' visitor, and the phone has to be on the recording machine in order to paint.

This is the new face of Delhi, where people come flocking each winter, not only from the U.S. and U.K. but also from Singapore, Hong Kong, Japan and Jakarta. Even artists from neighbouring countries like Nepal, Pakistan, Bangladesh and Sri Lanka now consider Delhi India's new cultural capital.

What's new in this new cultural capital? The page three phenomenon, where some long to be seen, and others are too shy, is here to stay. One fearfully watches for a familiar face behind the camera every time one steps into an artist's opening, or even a Reshma or Wadali brothers' recital. Diplomatic cards pour into artists' studios, committees beckon you, schools and colleges hope you will 'chief guest' their functions.

You do need a 48-hour day if you are to do your primary thing
– painting. You are lucky if you can.

This ride on the magic carpet that is Delhi can be heady but
exhausting, but the city itself brings you reprieve. Every unbearable
summer, it pushes you to the mountains, or back into your shell
where you can paint to your heart's content. Come to think of it,
one lifetime does not seem enough for all that you want to paint. So
much does this city offer.

There is the National Museum with its fabulous miniature and
sculpture collection, and every visit can trigger off fresh images in the
mind. There is the Crafts Museum where folk art flourishes. These
folk artists, who carry on generations of community traditions, have
few takers for their work in their own states. Delhi is their Mecca, but
they have to pay several visits before they get a chance to exhibit their
work in their two dream places – Dilli Haat and the Crafts Museum.
While both have done a lot to popularize folk art, it's obviously not
enough for the innumerable folk artists in India's villages.

Then, Delhi has the country's oldest, and perhaps, the only
contemporary museum in the country, the National Gallery of Modern
Art. Confined to Jaipur House, which refuses to expand, nearly 97%
of the collection is in storage, but one still makes repeated visits to see
the remaining 3%, so lovingly displayed by its new director. Though
plans for a new building were approved a decade ago, funds, we've
been told, are lacking. The sprawling Indira Gandhi National Centre
for Arts seems to be lying vacant these days, but at the India Habitat
Centre, there is a buzz of activity under its new art director, who has
come from Chandigarh. Nearby, Stein's spirit still presides quietly
over the old charm of the India International Centre.

And of course, there are my favourite monuments, which I
have visited thousands of times, and never tire of. The Bangla Sahib
gurdwara, the quiet, uninhabited air of the Damdama Sahib gurdwara,
the *dargah* of Nizamuddin Auliya where Amir Khusro also lies, Jamali
Kamali beyond the magnificent Qutub Minar, the dargah of Khwaja
Bakhtiar Kaki in Mehrauli, the feeling of space at the Old Fort and

Humayun's Tomb... I could go on. I especially like the little known Khirki Masjid, with its myriad arches, and nine clusters of nine domes on the roof, almost intact after five centuries. Tucked away behind clusters of tenements and choked streets is Chirag Dilli, where peacocks strut around tombs camouflaged with plastic waste. History struggles to breathe and be acknowledged in the fashionable and chic Hauz Khas village, while hoardings scream garish messages from the defenceless walls of Masjid Moth.

Will the coming generations know our quiet childhood in Chandni Chowk and the tears that rise to our eyes in Ferozeshah Kotla, Khooni Darwaza and the well in the Maulana Azad complex, where the spirits of martyrs whisper in despair at an increasingly violent and divided nation? A nation torn by contradictions, a nation that is fast forgetting the sacrifices made by martyrs as they dreamt of a free flag, fluttering on the ramparts of Red Fort. On every crowded street, there is one such relic from the past, struggling to breathe amid the tangle of ugly new constructions, TV antennae and cables.

Behind my house, the women of Shahpur Jat dry hundreds of dung cakes every day on the steel walls of a thermal power station skirting the oldest wall in Delhi, the remnants of Siri Fort. This strange, surreal mix of old and new triggered off a whole series of paintings for me, 'Between Dualities', where I collaborated and cosigned with a folk artist (erstwhile tattoo artist) who appropriates skin colour by actually coating cowdung diluted with water on paper.

In this series, his trees (that Delhi once had in abundance) are strangulated and embraced by neon trees.

Siri Fort wall, the oldest 13th century wall from where the Mongols were first defeated, never to come back, having conquered large parts of China, Europe and Asia, has been ruthlessly usurped by voracious builders and a banquet hall, in connivance with civic agents and government builders who treat Delhi's monuments as their personal fiefdom.

Laws that prevent encroachments within 100 metres of any monument are routinely flouted. All pleas and letters to the authorities fall on deaf ears; perhaps in the mad race for money, money and more money, people have become too callous to care anymore.

What is history then? We have no reverence for it in Delhi. And we have no reverence for the innumerable court injunctions against noise pollution through loudspeakers, amplifiers, construction activity, vehicular horns and crackers after 10 pm. For *baraats, jagraatas* and Punjabi pop, midnight is the magic hour. The noise may shatter your nerves, but any mention is taboo. Wealth must be on garish display at weddings, to the accompaniment of loud Punjabi pop, the same tunes which so easily adapt into praise of the almighty.

Delhi's citizens pray for sleep while others prey on their nerves. And no number of midnight calls to the police help. But did these help in 1984, when thousands were burnt alive in or outside their homes?

Delhi has a bloody history. You can smell it in post '84 Trilokpuri as you can in Tughlaqabad. But Delhi forgets and forgives, and carries on. It's the place of power, of all the manipulative chess games of grabbing more power, with the empty canopy of India Gate as one of the many reminders of its capacity for forgiveness, its irony, its nostalgia.

Phir bhi, kahaan jaoge Ghalib, Dilli ki galiyan chhorh ke?

Wither, the walled city

SATISH JACOB

AN international survey has recently pronounced New Delhi to be among the worst cities in the world to live in. That may well be. But in my childhood, Old Delhi was a glorious city, full of charm, vitality and a vibrant culture, a city that fully lived up to a Persian poet's description as 'paradise on earth'. The happiest days of my childhood during the 1950s were spent in the walled city (or Shahjahanabad) where I was born and my memories of paradise are still vivid, particularly of kite flying and pigeon racing and the distinctive culture that permeated our lives.

On Eid, the skies above Old Delhi would be full of purple, blue, green, black, orange and red kites, plain and patterned, small and big, flying high and low. Children's hearts would thrill when two kites got entangled in a *'painch'* or dog fight, a struggle that would be cut short by the sudden cry of *'woh kaata'* when the string of one of the kites was cut and it fluttered down in defeat. I was too small to fly kites myself but I watched teams engage in contests on the Ram Lila grounds and had a field day with my friends catching the vanquished kites as they descended. The best time was during the monsoon when the dark grey of the sky and whirling white clouds provided a dramatic backdrop.

I also remember the pigeon racing that happened in the mornings and evenings. No matter what the weather – burning hot winds, lashing rains or the chill of winter – the *kabutar wallahs* never failed to fly their pigeons from the rooftops while the whole area resounded to their cries of *'ha..koo.. aao'*. Hundreds of them would stud the sky, racing along, wings closed, moving like arrows across the sky.

Pigeon racing was an expensive hobby generally indulged in only by the rich and upper middle classes. Every Thursday, the Muslim sabbath, the who's who of Old Delhi came to the big square in front of Jama Masjid to buy prized pigeons from Iran and Afghanistan. A good pair would fetch as much as five rupees, a small fortune when you consider that a clerk's salary was about Rs 100 on which, moreover, he could lead a decent life with at least two servants and a comfortable house. One rupee would buy 40 kilos of wheat or four kilos of *desi ghee* and two paise could buy you a sumptuous meal of *paranthas* and meat curry. The level of comfort was high, so too was a feeling of abundance, which is why roadside stalls never charged anything for *dal*. It was served free with the meal.

It was possible to maintain a lifestyle befitting a nawab on a small income. Servants, whole squadrons of them, used to work for a household without any emoluments. They were regarded as part of the family and it was understood that the master of the house would take care of all their needs, including the marriage of their children. At the heart of the household stood the institution of the *mughlani* (senior housekeeper). She was traditionally a woman of high birth and, though technically an employee, held in high esteem by the entire family. A formidable presence in the house, she was governess, teacher and manager rolled into one. One of her tasks was to prepare the daughters of the family for their future role as wives by teaching them how to sew, cook, make lace and embroider. The *khansama* or cook also played a crucial role because people in Old Delhi loved to entertain and serve tenderly prepared delicacies to please the discerning palate of their gourmand friends. Even my father, who was not a nawab, held dinner parties at least twice a month and the preparations were both elaborate and painstaking.

The walled city was full of *havelis*. There are, of course, hardly any left now. The havelis abandoned by the Muslim aristocracy when it migrated to Pakistan were taken over either by Hindu refugees who had lost their homes in West Punjab or by the government. As a child I remember being struck by how vast they were; I do not exaggerate when I say that some had courtyards as big as football fields. In fact, as young boys, we regularly played cricket in the courtyard of a haveli owned by a family of *hakims* in Ballimaran.

The haveli where Zeenat Mahal, the favourite queen of the last Mughal emperor, Bahadur Shah Zafar, lived, is now being used as a big iron market; some families have also built their homes there. The old opulence has gone. The haveli belonging to the Englishman, James Skinner, in Gali Qasim Jaan had a courtyard in which he kept elephants and horses. Mirza Ghalib lived in Gali Qasim Jaan and so did Shamsuddin Khan, the Nawab of Loharu, who was hanged at the age of 25 for the murder of William Fraser, the Resident of Delhi, the virtual ruler of the city. Shamsuddin hired an assassin who waylaid Fraser one winter evening when he was returning to his *kothi* outside Kashmere Gate. Shamsuddin was later hanged at Kashmere Gate, watched by hundreds of people. It is said that he went to the gallows with great dignity and composure. Mirza Ghalib's reputation, however, did not fare so well. He was criticized for choosing to testify against Shamsuddin even though his wife was a Loharu.

All the havelis of the well-to-do had a similar layout. A massive gate and a high boundary wall were two obvious external features. Inside, the walls were so deep that niches cut into them were large enough to be used as rooms by the servants or palanquin bearers. The inner courtyard invariably had a small garden with fountains. Lining the four sides of the courtyard were rooms, arches and colonades. This was the men's area, known as the *diwan khana* or *mardana*. The mardana was connected with the *zenana* by a small door and corridor which too had its own garden and courtyard. A diwan khana and zenana were indications of a man's position in society, however modest in size and accoutrements they may have been. Certain trappings, such as palanquins – the traditional mode of transport for the women of illustrious families – and the *kahars* who carried them, were also essential.

Before the 1930s, men travelled in bullock carts or in horsedrawn carriages known as *ikka*s that were really a kind of *rath* covered with a canopy. Rickshaws, bicycles, *tongas* and trams came later in the 1940s. I remember travelling with my father in a tonga to see a movie at the nearest cinema house. There were about seven or eight cinema houses in Old Delhi. People called them 'bioscope'. The more proletarian members of society called them *mandwa*. For some reason, the old picture halls were hardly ever called by their proper names – the Ritz, the Novelty or Kumar Talkies (which incidentally still stands in Chandni Chowk and has recently been renovated). Instead, they were known by the area in which they were situated. So Kumar Talkies was *patharwala* and Jagat was *machliwala*. And the movies were advertized by hoardings on wheels pushed by two men around the busy streets of Chandni Chowk, Khari Baoli, Urdu Bazaar, Nai Sadak, Dariba, Matia Mahal and Hauz Qazi. Unknown in those days, M.F. Hussain could be seen painting movie hoardings on Esplanade Road. Gramophone players and radios were introduced around the same time. Those who were the first to see the heavy black discs called them *tawas* and the name stuck.

The only wide roads in Old Delhi were in Chandni Chowk, Hauz Qazi, Khari Baoli and Daryaganj. Perhaps the passage of time expands the sense of space experienced in childhood but certainly during the hot afternoons when we played cricket in the small streets in front of our homes, the alleys and narrow lanes of the neighbourhood appeared perfectly wide to us. We had seen nothing else, after all. And perhaps they felt spacious because the population in 1947 was little more than 150,000. In fact, walking home from school during winter evenings was quite scary because there were hardly any people on the streets. Street lights were virtually non-existent and few people had electricity.

In earlier decades, before the advent of electricity, the streets were illuminated with huge torches known as *mashals*. The well-to-do also lit up their havelis with mashals; the poor made do with *diyas* or earthen lamps. I remember the streets being quiet and deserted (except for the days when *mehfils* or literary gatherings were organized) as I walked home after an evening at a friend's place. Yet, most people felt safe walking on the roads at night because crime was rare.

Summer was glorious, filled with bliss. Families went for picnics to places as far as Qutub and Okhla but my friends and I were quite happy pursuing adventures nearer home. We'd go in groups for a swim in the Jamuna and then gorge on the melons and kakris we stole from the fields near the river. The countryside outside the walled city was full of orchards and gardens. Further away, Punjabi Bagh, Shalimar Bagh, Gulabi Bagh and even Jor Bagh enjoyed an abundance of trees. We would feast on loquat, jamun, mangoes, mulberries and ber and most of the time the good-natured gardeners did not mind our plunders. The banks of the Jamuna were surrounded by fields that were our favourite hunting grounds because of the antelopes and wild boar that roamed the area in hundreds. It was such a complete and self-enclosed universe for those who lived there that everyone referred to the parts of Delhi outside the walled city as *jungle bar*.

We would also stroll in groups to Nizamuddin to hear the *qawwalis* at the annual *urs* marking a saint's death or birth anniversary. The urs were great occasions for hearing the best *qawwals* in the country. I had the good fortune to hear Habib Painter sing at the *dargah* of Hazrat Nizamuddin.

The tradition of urs and *mushairas* were the vestiges of a more spectacular and stupendous past – Mughal civilization at its zenith. If I loved the Old Delhi I grew up in, the people around me made it clear that it was nothing compared to the splendours they either recalled, or had read about, of the city's earlier imperial glory. If the old families of Old Delhi preserved the cultural traditions by continuing

to hold urs and mushairas in their homes, it was as much a homage to
Mughal culture and refinement. But unlike the mushairas in homes,
the emperor and nobles held them on a much larger scale at the Red
Fort or in their mansions. These were great social occasions, talked
about for weeks and graced by the presence of some of the best Urdu
poets of the times such as Mir, Momin, Ghalib, Zauq and Dard.

The *mahaul* during Mughal times was the exact antithesis of
the decay and decline that characterize Old Delhi today. The streets
and alleys pulsated with life, beauty, grace and a refinement that
overwhelmed visitors. This was a culture that knew it was splendid
and proud of its achievements. The tea houses in the walled city were
frequented by intellectuals, poets, royal courtiers and scholars who
would spend hours discussing the topics of the day. It was not just
Indians who were enchanted by the street life, culture and shops; the
city's fame spread far and wide. Chandni Chowk, for example, came
to be regarded as one of the greatest trading centres and bazaars of
the Orient, particularly for jewellery, a place where merchants from
China, Arabia and Persia would congregate to buy and sell precious
stones, perfumes and fabulous brocades.

After the Mutiny, of course, many prominent Muslim families
fell on bad times as the British wreaked their terrible retribution
on perceived collaborators or sympathizers. The fortunes of many
plummeted; the fall in social status was often greater. The members of
some former Mughal families resorted to earning a living from selling
racing pigeons. Some princesses ended up marrying commoners or
begging on the streets because their entire families had been wiped
out in the bloodbath that followed the Mutiny and the families and
acquaintances that remained were simply too frightened to take them
in for fear of British retaliation.

Today's mad congestion was unknown then, naturally enough,
but it was also unknown when I was growing up. Of course, areas
such as the one where Old Delhi railway station is now located and
the area between Company Garden and Kashmere Gate were quite
heavily populated. But somehow the canals and the foliage of the tree-

lined roads imparted a sense of peace and order. For example, there was a big pond between the Town Hall and Nai Sadak in Chandni Chowk where, later on, the Clock Tower was built. And a canal flowed from the Red Fort to Fatehpuri Mosque with gigantic mango and jamun trees lining the way. In the hot summer, bamboo poles would be fixed on both sides of the pavements in Chandni Chowk with vast swathes of brightly coloured cloth stretched across them to provide shade for pedestrians.

But the sights, sounds and smells of this colourful outdoor life were shrouded in mystery for the women of the zenana where life went on, month after month, year after year, with a relentless monotony relieved only by the occasional visit from an aunt, cousin or some relative. Women rarely went out anywhere. Since the city was predominantly Muslim, *purdah* was observed by all women. Somehow, women devised their own entertainment, joking and gossiping among themselves or with the servants and looking forward to festivals, parties and weddings. The boredom was so phenomenal that some women would organize weddings of their dolls and host parties for the families of the 'bride' and 'bridegroom'. If nothing else, it gave these cloistered women a chance to dress up and look forward to something. Sometimes *nautch* girls would be invited to sing and dance on special occasions.

Unable to participate in the external world, women relied on their own elaborate intelligence networks to find out what was happening in the city – who was marrying whom, whose child was misbehaving, whose parents were being neglected or whose husband was philandering. Since respectable women rarely went shopping in the market, merchants took their wares to them. So, apart from bringing fruit, sweetmeats, bangles and clothes to the women inside their havelis, the female merchandize sellers would also convey to them gossip and news from the wider society otherwise inaccessible.

This lack of education and knowledge meant most women were markedly superstitious. They tended to blame evil spirits for virtually every ailment and would call mendicants or holy men, asking for amulets and charms to keep the evil spirits away. It was common for people in the walled city to describe dust storms during the summer as 'the marriage' of *jinns* or evil spirits. Old women would quickly put a broom under the leg of a bed in the hope that it would keep the *jinns* away. Women were gullible victims of quacks and their cures. I remember some who visited my neighbourhood claiming that burying the blood of a cockerel was a wonderful way of exorcising ghosts.

Despite the dependence on holy men and traditional forms of medicine, western-style education had nevertheless started making inroads towards the end of the 19th century. St. Stephen's College was started in 1881 and Hindu College a few years later. Both Muslims and Hindus needed much cajoling to persuade them to send their daughters to school or college. Queen Mary's School, set up by Christian missionaries in 1911, was one of the first school for girls to be established in northern India. Initially located near the Jama Masjid (it was later moved to Tis Hazari when more space was required), its exceptionally high walls were built out of deference to Muslim parental anxiety that no prying eyes should get a glimpse of the young girls who were, in any case, accompanied by chaperones who waited in one part of the building until school was over.

The daughters of the Muslim aristocracy and the upper middle classes began attending school, arriving in elegant horse-drawn carriages. Their attendance marked a revolution in social customs, a radical break with the tradition of keeping girls at home and in a state of ignorance. For boys too, education became more popular as parents realized that it could help their sons find secure government jobs and improve their matrimonial prospects. Those families who refused to embrace education and stuck to feudal attitudes gradually but inexorably fell behind the times.

The onset of western education also brought about changes in lifestyle: men began to wear western clothes; European-style furniture was introduced in homes; eating out in restaurants and hotels became acceptable; the cigarette pushed the *hookah* into obscurity; *sherbet* and *falooda* gave way to soda lemonade; horse-drawn carriages were forced to give right of way to motor cars; and instead of buying havelis, affluent people bought houses in the new residential areas of Civil Lines and New Delhi. The walled city began to change. People increasingly began to seek jobs in government offices and commercial establishments. Traders became important and respectable citizens, as did factory owners. In direct proportion to their earlier social ascendancy, the former nobility now fell into decline and was relegated to the fringes.

Almost all senior officials were British in the decades before independence. Some Indians held them in great awe. My father would tell me, without irony, that any Indian summoned by a British officer would instinctively feel nervous and half-guilty as though he were a schoolboy being hauled up by a policeman; he would adjust his cap, button up his coat and look anxiously at the *sahib's* face to decipher what exactly lay in store. It came as no surprise, therefore, that a newspaper in the 1930s offered the following advice to Indians on how to conduct themselves when called to the home or office of an Englishman:

'Do not go to visit an Englishman before 10 a.m. and after 1 p.m. If another visitor comes then leave. Take permission to leave. The British do not have the custom of telling you to go, so do not wait for him to say something, just leave. If the lady of the house is present then wish her respectfully. If the lady extends her hand to shake yours, only then shake hands with her. Do not comment on her looks. Do not tell her your problems or of any other persons, only if she asks may you tell her. Very often Indians say things that annoy the British, so be careful.

Dress properly, do not wear a cap or loose pyjama... do not under any circumstances talk of personal and family matters. Sometimes elderly people ask questions as to how many rooms there are in the kothi or what is the person's salary or if he knows so and so. This is considered extremely improper. Apart from this Indians have the habit of asking sahibs for letters of recommendation for friends or acquaintances – this is the reason they do not want to meet Indians.'

The glorious heritage of Old Delhi makes the decline of the past 50 years all the more distressing for people like me who lived and grew up in this enchanted, gentle and civilized city. The power never failed. Running water was available 24 hours a day. The air was clean. The streets of the bazaars were sprinkled with water during the summer afternoons to keep the dust levels down. That Old Delhi is now a distant dream. It could not have survived unchanged; it had to meet the challenges of the modern world and adopt, but it failed to emerge from this enterprise successfully because it was let down by the bankruptcy of political leadership and administration.

Yet, it hasn't been for lack of administration or management. Ironically, until the late 1950s, only a deputy commissioner administered Delhi. Now there is a lieutenant governor, chief minister, state assembly, mayor, municipal corporation, and a Delhi Development Authority. But everywhere corruption and chaos prevail. Everything, from roads to sewers, is choking. Old Delhi is dying. Mir Taqi Mir once said, *'Dilli jo ek shahr tha aalam mein intikhaab/Hum rehne wale hain usi ujre dayar ke* – There was a city, famed throughout the world/Where dwelt the chosen spirits of the age/Delhi its name, fairest among the fair/Fate looted it and laid it desolate/And to that ravaged city I belong.'

If the equally great poet Zauq were to see what has become of Old Delhi now, he would not have asked, as he once did in a famous couplet, *'Kaun jaye Zauq Dilli ki galiyan chor ke'* – Who would wish to leave the lanes of Delhi and live elsewhere? Instead, he would ask: who could bear to stay?

Learning to belong

PAVAN K. VARMA

I DO not 'belong' to Delhi, so why should Delhi belong to me? Can a person belong to any one city, and, can a city belong to any person? A city like Delhi symbolizes a vast anonymity. An individual is part of a personalized world. Where do the two meet? What is that cross-section at which the city loses its objectivity to become for an individual an extension of his self? And, what is that point at which an individual transcends his own personal world to embrace the larger objectivity of a city?

These are difficult questions to answer. I was not born in Delhi. My parents were not born in Delhi. My grandparents were not born in Delhi. How then do I claim this city to be my own? I first came to Delhi as a one-year old child in 1954 when my father, who was in government, was posted to the new capital of India. My first memories are of growing up in Man Nagar, now called Rabindra Nagar, a residential area only inhabited by other government servants. Man Nagar was then almost at the periphery of New Delhi. Outside its gates was the seductive wilderness of Lodhi Gardens.

New Delhi was a small city. It was the city of Lutyens and Baker, largely homogeneous, a bureaucratic city symbolizing power rather than money. Its inhabitants were few, the municipal pressures on them fewer. When the first traffic lights were erected, people were amused. Raj Path was then still remembered as Kingsway, Queen Mary's Avenue had not yet been christened Pandit Pant Marg, and a new name for Connaught Place was decades away. Absorbed in its new-found importance, New Delhi was essentially more a hierarchy than a city, presided over by the privileged layer of senior bureaucrats, established politicians and old money.

In my early years, I do not recall a visit to the old city, except to catch a train from the Delhi railway station. Shahjahanabad, defined by the towering minarets of Jama Masjid and the ramparts of Red Fort, and distinctive for its labyrinthine alleys, *galis* and *kuchas*, was opaque to me. This was both understandable and (for me) ironic. Understandable, because New Delhi stood as much for continuity as a complete rupture with the past. The continuity was self-evident. New Delhi was one more city in an unbroken history that had made Delhi the city of several empires and kingdoms. The rupture was less proclaimed, but equally transparent.

New Delhi was built to expressly break its association with the older city ruled by the Mughals. When in 1911, it was decided to shift the British capital to Delhi, both Lutyen and Baker initially wanted to integrate the old city with the new in a manner that would allow the former to retain its essential character and yet stem the chaotic commercialization and industrialization that was destroying it. As historian Narayani Gupta writes in *Delhi Between Two Empires* (OUP 1997): 'A long processional avenue was planned from the fort through Delhi Gate, past a park and a boulevard with the houses of Indian princes lining both sides. Another was to cut through the side of Jama Masjid from the proposed King Edward Memorial Park, and bear southwestward to the new railway station, whence another road was to lead to Kashmiri Gate.'

These roads were never built. Thus it was that the sharp contrast between an expansive residential area and an over-congested commercial slum was formalized and perpetuated. Shahjahanabad was deliberately left to die as a neglected memory of a rejected past. And New Delhi was created as a 'new' statement of imperial intention, even if its architects, in an act of benign indulgence, took some architectural motifs of the past and incorporated them in the red sandstone buildings on Raisina Hill.

The irony is that my first serious cerebral discovery of Delhi had little to do with New Delhi, where I had grown up, but with Old Delhi, which I had never visited as a child. In the early '80s, I began to research the life of Mirza Ghalib. The book that finally emerged (Penguin 1998) was really a portrait of the old city in the 19th century using Ghalib's life as a focus. I have often wondered why I wrote this book. I had studied history but was not a historian. I loved Urdu but had no formal training in literature. But I was fascinated by the period in which Ghalib lived.

The Mughal empire was then in its death throes, although the British, the *de facto* rulers, still pretended to bow before the last Mughal emperor, Bahadur Shah Zafar, whose writ did not run beyond the Red Fort. It was a period when Delhi went through the trauma of 1857. It was a time when, within its wall, Urdu poetry came into its own. It was a phase of great cultural achievement and unprecedented political decline.

This period fascinated me but I hardly knew the city in which it unfolded. I was a product of the wide boulevards of New Delhi, not the narrow lanes of Shahjahanabad. My exposure was to the bureaucratic insularities and certitudes of the new city, not the genteel impoverishment and neglect of the old. Yet, my first emotional umbilical chord with Delhi was through the many years happily researching its previous incarnation: Shahjahanabad.

The biography of Ghalib led to a second book on the old city: *Mansions at Dusk – The Havelis of Old Delhi*. My research on Ghalib had taken me innumerable times to Shahjahanabad. On such visits,

I was able to see the plight of the old city. I was witness to the relentless destruction of a habitat which was once home to a cultured nobility, who lived in beautiful havelis, the end product of a definitive architectural tradition. I was deeply concerned that if no attempt was made to chronicle what the city once was through the little that remained of its past, soon there would be nothing remaining in the present to reconstruct that past. Thus began the idea of the book on the havelis of Delhi. Sondeep Shankar, a well known photographer, became a ready ally. Every weekend, for more than a year, Sondeep and I would travel to the old city and marvel afresh at its many seductions and the pace at which they were being destroyed.

The Havelis of Old Delhi is a sad book. It helped chronicle the lifestyle and idiom of a bygone era, but it could not stem the indifference of the powers that be. Meanwhile, New Delhi continued to grow phenomenally, far beyond the expectations of any town planner. Undoubtedly, New Delhi will always remain the apex bureaucratic citadel and the unquestioned political capital of India. In this sense, it can never change.

But over the years, it has become much more than just a city of politicians and bureaucrats. Today, it is a commercial city too. A new middle class, confident of its entrepreneurial skills, has made it a home. Industrial units have begun to dot its suburbs. Money power has begun to jostle with political power, and very often the two are inextricably linked. New residential areas have come up far beyond the periphery of Lutyen's vision. People from all over India have made the city their home. The old middle class, monetarily frayed at the edges, has given way to the new rich. The expanding city has swallowed up entire villages. For the first time, it has spread its tentacles across the Jamuna. I recall my father in the early '60s trying desperately to locate Defence Colony. When we built our home in Vasant Vihar in the early '70s, taxi drivers would refuse to go beyond Moti Bagh. I will never forget a scooter-*walla* turning to me and saying: *Kahan jangal mein le ja rahe hain?*

I remember too that to catch my school bus, I had to cycle to Moti Bagh since the bus did not venture beyond Moti Bagh. Today, New Delhi's residential suburbs extend for 20 kilometres beyond Vasant Vihar which has become a mainstream residential area. There are other things that have changed in New Delhi. I distinctly remember the pleasure of sleeping out under a star-bedecked sky during summer. There were no mosquitoes. We never slept under mosquito nets. There was no water shortage. I have no memory of any power cuts.

Like its newer incarnation, Old Delhi too is a picture of both change and continuity. In spite of the onslaught on the basic character of the city, its essential features have not changed. Shahjahanabad is a historical city. It can be mutilated but it cannot completely obliterate its past. Undoubtedly, from a gracious feudal city inhabited by not very many more than a 100,000 people, it is now a commercial slum. The lovely Nahar-i-Bihisht once flowed through the centre of a streetlined avenue called Chandni Chowk. Today that street has become so crowded that one can hardly walk.

There was a time when the old city was so quiet that the 'tuk... tuk...tuk' sound of the *karigar* (artisan) beating silver and gold into *vark* (thin foils) could be heard clearly within a radius of a furlong. Today over the din of traffic and small factories running lathes, one has to shout to converse. Not too long ago (in fact in the earlier part of the last century), through the summer months at about five in the evening, when the worst heat of the day was on the wane, a bullock cart laden with water would start its leisurely, water-sprinkling journey from the Town Hall, passing by the Fountain Chowk, Jama Masjid, Chawri Bazar, Hauz Qazi and other important areas. The entire city would wake up around this time from its leisurely afternoon siesta. Today, innumerable industrial establishments work through the night, be it summer or winter. The old city is physically there, but only as a settlement without a soul.

My third book on Delhi (Harper Collins 1993) had its origins in a request by Raghu Rai, the well known photographer. Raghu had been photographing the city for many years. He asked me to write a text to accompany his photographs. I wrote the text in first person, as a *sutradhar* who was in Delhi when Indraprastha was built, and who also was there to witness the first British viceroy enter the newly built Viceregal Lodge atop Raisina Hill in 1931.

The narrative has a parallel theme. It begins with dawn and ends at dusk. The opportunity to write about the city through a highly personalized and subjective prism reinforced my sense of kinship with it. Perhaps for entirely irrational reasons, I now began to look at Delhi not only as an object of research but as something personal and familiar, a process not very different from a car acquiring a human personality after long years in a family. For me the city became an individual with a soul, a territory with a personalized story, a persona which I could relate to at a private meeting point. This private world, of man and city, is inseparable now from my relationship with Delhi.

The *Millennium Book on New Delhi,* which I helped edit, was my first project specifically on New Delhi. It was Home Minister L.K. Advani's idea to have such a book. He felt that New Delhi had grown and evolved from a small colonial city built by the British as a statement of their imperial might, to a cosmopolitan metropolis presiding over the destiny of a free India and the world's largest democracy. He wanted a book on the self-conscious personality of New Delhi.

I vividly recall the first meeting on the planning of this book which took place on a cold December morning in 1998 in the ornate conference room of the Home Ministry in the North Block under the chairmanship of the then Home Secretary (and the chief editor of the book) B.P. Singh. I was the youngest among those who had been called to give ideas on the book. Not surprisingly I was asked to draw a draft outline on the structure of the book. The outline was written on a golden afternoon on the last day of that year during a holiday in Simla. The book, which had contributions from Khushwant Singh, the late Professor Ravinder Kumar, Sunita Kohli, Mark Tully, Madhu

Jain and others, was published by Oxford University Press and released by the President of India in February 2001 at perhaps the only book launch ever held at the Ashoka Hall of the Rashtrapati Bhavan.

If I sit down to draw a balance sheet on my association with Delhi, do I have no more to show than an involvement in writing four books on the city? I know the relationship is much deeper. I do not know if the city belongs to me, but I do know that I have no other place I can call home. Even though I was not born in this city, I grew up in it. It provided the background to my childhood, and the foundation on which I structured my later life. It is the city where I met my wife. It is the city where my children were born.

My forefathers came from a small district town near Varanasi called Ghazipur. A poet so recalled his association with Ghazipur:

Ye galian mera bachpan yahan se guzra hai/Kahanian jo suni thi yahan pe soti hain.

(My childhood has passed by in these alleyways/The stories I heard then continue to sleep here).

Perhaps that is my bond with Delhi. And I know for sure that even if I remain a perpetual aspirant to 'belong' to it, for my children, who were born here, there can be no other home.

Resident alien

AJOY BOSE

CONSIDERING how much I now detest the city, my first memories of Delhi are actually quite amiable. In the early '60s, visiting Delhi as a 10 year old to attend a cousin's wedding, I remember the city as a quaint diversion from the relentless urban hustle bustle of my home in Calcutta. The streets were wide and empty and the lack of clatter of trams and buses was a pleasant surprise. Even more surprising was the predominance of bicycles on the road, many of them mounted by ladies wearing strange tight-fitting outfits which I later learnt were Sadhna style *salwar kameez* suits. For a Calcutta boy who had never before seen Indian women wear anything else but sarees or ride bicycles, it was the highlight of my first encounter with the capital of the country.

I returned to the city nearly a decade later, only to find that its old world charm was fast fading. This time I was more than a boy attending a wedding. As an undergraduate at St. Stephen's College, I had enough time to discover that Delhi, by the start of the '70s, had become rough and unruly, far removed from my boyhood memories. The streets were still wide but the clatter of traffic had increased by leaps and bounds. There were no trams but the buses were mobile monsters which held unimaginable terrors for those on the roads as well the passengers within.

Apart from engaging in a race to death with cars, auto-rickshaws, cycles and sundry pedestrians, Delhi buses provided a remarkable ritual celebrating the horrors of bus travel. It was not just overcrowding – buses in Calcutta carried far more numbers. The first problem here was that buses usually halted way beyond the bus stop, provoking a mad stampede of passengers. Second, by design or accident, doors of Delhi buses in the '70s were tortuously narrow, almost half the width of their Calcutta counterparts. Most importantly, there was still no notion of a queue which was invented in Delhi only during the Emergency (perhaps one of the few gains of those 19 months). It was an amazing spectacle to see passengers hurling themselves simultaneously at narrow doors with the conductor trying his best to push them out.

The damsels in salwar kameez suits riding bicycles, who had so caught my boyish imagination, had completely disappeared from the roads of Delhi. They were trapped inside Delhi buses suffering a fate worse than death. I was used to Calcutta buses where the conductor, when ladies got in or out, led a chorus crying 'ladies are coming', which warned male passengers to press back, however crowded the space, to avoid any physical contact with feminine flesh. To my horror I found that on a Delhi bus, exactly the opposite happened. Most male passengers as well as the conductor seemed determined to have close encounters with the feminine kind. Indeed, such was my Calcutta upbringing and so crude were the advances made on the hapless lady passengers that I had repeated physical scraps on my first few bus journeys in Delhi, much to the surprise of both victims and perpetrators.

Meanwhile, the stately architecture of St. Stephen's College with its academic elegance (or was it elegant academics?) offered a sanctuary away from the rest of the city. Even the unfamiliar and wholly obnoxious ritual of ragging could not mar the brunches of mince and scrambled eggs at the cafeteria or lolling around the quadrangle lawns in front of the residential blocks. Behind the back gate of the college lay Miranda House, inviting fantasies involving women who never had to board Delhi buses.

At St. Stephen's the rest of the city, including adjoining colleges except Miranda House, simply did not exist. My friendship with a leading wrestler from the college across the road (though it did save me from ragging) was openly frowned upon by my peers in Stephen's. Coming from Calcutta where snobs were considered a lowly species, this was my first encounter with social snobbery. On the other hand, when the riff-raff outside did impose themselves on college life, I found Stephanians strangely submissive. I still remember in my very first fortnight in Stephen's a fellow student being dragged out by the scruff of his neck from the packed college dining hall by just three hoods from a college across the road. The absence of protest or resistance from the more than 300 Stephanians present left me completely baffled.

I was sent for my undergraduate studies to St. Stephen's to escape the Naxalite turmoil in the colleges of Calcutta. Having rejected 'dictatorship of the proletariat' in my precocious reading bouts in school and regarding myself more of a liberal than an extremist, I very much doubt that I would have displayed any inclination towards Naxalism had I stayed on in Calcutta. But the culture shock in Delhi, whether on its buses or within the ivory towers of Stephen's, may well have triggered off unknown impulses inside me. Moreover, the few peers in college I did like belonged to the minority Naxalite group in Stephen's and it did not take me long to embrace the romance of the extreme Left. I have happy memories of marching down Mall Road singing revolutionary songs with my newfound comrades on our way to eat bun *makhan* at the *dhaba* in Khyber Pass. However, a series of outrageous escapades in college culminating in a fight with a RSS goon (my first encounter with the organization) finally provoked the college authorities to clamp a lock on my hostel room, cutting short my stint at St. Stephen's as well my university studies.

I left Delhi shortly afterwards to make revolution in the Bihar countryside but not before an educative stop-over in a city slum. This was my first experience of living in a slum although there was a large slum colony right next to my house in North Calcutta. There were five of us from St. Stephen's cramped inside a tiny airless room whose only ventilation came from the open door. Fortunately, it was winter and in any case we were much too fired up with fresh revolutionary zeal to care about our sordid surroundings. The only serious problem lay in conducting our morning ablutions in a ditch outside – yet another first for all of us.

The problem became particularly vexatious if one got the urge at night when stray dogs prowled the slum colony. One night, a comrade who considered himself superior to others because of his supposedly better grasp of Marxist dialectics (he is now a bigwig in some international agency abroad), was desperate enough to venture out. A few minutes later we could hear the barking of dogs in the distance. We could not but speculate on the plight of our senior comrade if set upon by the slum dogs. True enough, the barking got louder and louder till suddenly he burst through the door frothing at the mouth and naked from the waist downwards. Close behind him was a pack of snarling dogs straight out of a scene in *Uncle Tom's Cabin*. Our gusts of laughter as we rolled on the floor got even louder when our hapless dialectical expert complained bitterly about the lack of comradely sympathy. Many months later in Bihar as the revolution collapsed around our heads, recalling this ludicrous episode of our life in a Delhi slum would still evoke considerable mirth.

I was back in Delhi less than three years later, recruited from a failed revolution by Aruna Asaf Ali, a revolutionary firebrand in the days of the freedom struggle and widow of the capital's first mayor. Arunaji, who published a pro-Soviet leftwing newspaper, *Patriot* and a magazine, *Link*, magnanimously offered a college dropout like me the position of a trainee reporter. My monthly stipend was just 300 rupees but I had seen enough hard times by then to live in Delhi on this pathetic sum. I was fortunate to find at 80 rupees a month, accommodation up on the roof of a government quarter in

Lodhi Colony. The room was fairly large with three walls, the fourth made of wooden planks (government regulations did not allow the construction of a full fledged pucca *barsati* room). The roof was completely private surrounded by high walls. One could have a bath, smoke, dope and even fornicate out in the open. The only problem was that on winter nights, it did get somewhat chilly with the wind whistling through the large gaps on the wooden planked wall. To my misfortune, my first winter in Lodhi Colony saw temperatures plummet to near zero degree centigrade for several nights running, mercilessly exposing my lack of a proper bed or bedding. After three sleepless nights, I turned in wearing every stitch of clothing that I owned, and slept like a log.

Food was provided by Jolly Mess, a local Bengali chummery which served fish twice a day and special mutton or chicken lunches on Sundays for an incredible 100 rupees a month. Which meant that after paying for my room and food, I was still left with more than a 100 rupees – enough for bus journeys and Charminar fags. I was all set to discover the world of journalism on Bahadur Shah Zafar Marg, Delhi's Fleet Street. My chief editor was Edatata Narayanan, an eccentric genius who obsessively combatted the forces of American capitalism and its minions in India. The newspaper's editorial policy was unabashedly partisan, supporting the CPI and Left Congress at a time when Indira Gandhi was still in the pro-Soviet mode. But the newspaper's approach to international and domestic politics did not concern me. I was far too busy pursuing the crime beat which each day introduced me to a fresh facet of the city.

The squalid shanty towns of East and Outer Delhi, paunchy crooked cops in betel juice stained police stations, social angularities of the Muslim ghetto around Jama Masjid, Tihar Jail with its cons and dope pushers, call girl rackets in public sector hotels – an endless kaleidoscope of new faces and places provided me writing material. My peers were hardboiled investigative city reporters, poorly paid and shabbily dressed. Most were men and the few women in the profession shared the same single-minded hunger for news. There was little glamour in Delhi journalism those days and the brief advent of a chauffeur driven lady reporter wearing diamonds and lipstick, I remember, created quite a diversion.

Then came the summer of 1975 and everything changed. The day before Emergency was imposed, I had been assigned my first major political story – a public rally at the Ramlila Maidan addressed by Jayaprakash Narayan. Next morning, much to my disappointment, no newspapers were at the doorstep. On my way to Bahadur Shah Zafar Marg, I had no inkling what had happened till I entered the newspaper office and a grim-faced colleague warned, 'Keep your mouth shut, Emergency has been declared.' Inside the darkened office which was without electricity, it took some time for me to grasp the enormity of events sweeping the capital, including the arrest of thousands of politicians and the imposition of censorship heralded by the snapping of power lines to newspaper offices. As we sat devastated in the dark only the chief editor seemed happy, cackling about how the rightwing had got its comeuppance. Later we went to Indira Gandhi's residence where vast rented crowds, including a large band of eunuchs, shouted slogans supporting the Emergency.

It is amazing to recall in these days of VVIP security that even the day after the government had put the entire Opposition behind bars, anyone could walk right up to the gates of the prime minister's house without being checked. The days, weeks and months that followed were indeed a nightmare. There was so much to report but not a word appeared in newspapers. Homes smashed by bulldozers, old people and teenagers castrated in sterilization camps, the bloodbath at Turkman Gate, student leaders abducted by policemen from the JNU campus. It is difficult to describe the frustration of not being able to see a single line in print even as my notebooks kept filling up with sensational news.

I was relegated to covering boring functions organized by embassies and cultural organizations belonging to the socialist bloc, where apart from disseminating the usual communist propaganda, sycophant Congress ministers were given an opportunity to drone on about the gains of the Emergency. The North Koreans were

particularly active and before long I was sick at the very mention
of the great leader Kim Il Sung and the Juche idea. The audience at
these functions mainly consisted of hired crowds from Delhi slums
brought by Congress leaders at piecemeal rates. I remember one North
Korean function when a last minute wrangling over rates caused a
commotion in the hall. It was difficult to explain to anxious North
Korean diplomats asking whether the protests were against their great
leader and the Juche idea that the fuss was about money and not
ideology.

Meanwhile, my chief editor was getting increasingly eccentric
and paranoid. One winter night, he announced to me that a trained
CIA agent had sneaked into the office and I was to immediately ask
the authorities to have him arrested. I rushed out to find a wretched
homeless fellow taking shelter from the cold outside and had to
shoo him away quickly before he could be charged with espionage.
The chief editor soon fell out with the Emergency regime in a fit
of characteristic truculence. Having been the only editor to openly
support the Emergency, he now went to the opposite extreme,
blacking out Sanjay Gandhi's photographs and actively encouraging
us to break censorship laws. One night a frenzied mob of Congress
goons arrived to burn down the office and it took a combination of
bluster and negotiating skills to get rid of them.

The nightmare vanished as suddenly as it had emerged. The
denouement and collapse of the Emergency regime ushered in a period
of rejoicing and hope overnight. My notebooks of unprinted news
blossomed into a book on Delhi under Emergency released by none
other than the hero of the Emergency, George Fernandes. It was a
good time to be a political journalist in Delhi. The dictatorship had
been replaced by a circus of squabbling politicians who leaked news
like the monsoon skies. My new job as the Delhi bureau chief of
the country's largest weekly, *Sunday*, as well as India correspondent
for the London *Guardian*, took me to ministerial chambers, political
party offices and of course, Parliament, where polemical debate had
resurfaced after a long gap.

In those heady days, I also found true love. We courted intensely alternating between the café at Triveni theatre and the open air Rambles restaurant in Connaught Place. Soon we were married and ensconced in a wonderful Defence Colony barsati with living cum dining room, bedroom, lovely terrace and a servant's quarter, all for 750 rupees. We even had a full time *khansama* who came for a mere 300 rupee monthly salary. Oh, those happy evenings, as we downed rum after rum sitting out on the roof and listening to the Rolling Stones. Occasionally, we would stroll down to Moet's restaurant in the market and share a plate of *seekh kebabs*, one *dal makhni* and two *naans* for exactly 10 rupees, including a rupee tip for the waiter.

The '80s marked the return of the Congress. Soon after the Gandhis came back to power, our Defence Colony barsati was burgled. It had to be coincidence but my friends were convinced that it was a return compliment from Sanjay and his friends for my book. Anyway, he himself was gone within a few months, starting the tragic jinx of violent deaths in the family. We moved from the barsati to a bungalow on Amrita Shergill Marg owned by my wife's parents who were abroad. With diplomats and business magnates as our neighbours, I was left wondering about the distance I had travelled from my room at the top in Lodhi Colony in less than a decade. Our first daughter was soon born amidst some drama since the doctor who was supposed to deliver her vanished at the most critical moment to keep a hair-dresser's appointment. After rushing back at the last minute with shampoo in her hair, she appalled my wife by apologizing that she had delivered a girl and enquiring whether I would be really disappointed. Perambulating our daughter in a pram around the adjoining Lodhi Gardens, we initiated a morning relationship with the picturesque gardens which has continued to this day, two decades later.

Indira Gandhi's assassination and the carnage afterwards jolted my domesticated idyll on Amrita Shergill Marg. Near my favourite taxi stand at Press Club, I watched helplessly as one of the drivers was tossed alive into a bonfire. The goons who went on rampage were of a different species than the ones I knew during the Emergency.

Spawned in the deconstructed world of resettlement colonies dotting the borders of Delhi, they were not only much meaner but also completely apolitical. The city was changing and getting even uglier.

I returned in the early '90s to live in Defence Colony and found that the '80s consumerist boom had changed the place beyond recognition. My old *panwala* now owned a general provisions store and two cars as well. Fancy restaurants with even fancier prices and shops bursting with foreign goods swamped the market. In its narrow confines, teenage louts raced their cars at breakneck speed playing loud music to impress girls wearing lots of lipstick and little else. In the decade that has followed, all these trends have magnified manifold. As has the number of five star hotels, shopping malls and page three parties elsewhere in the city.

If, despite all this, we still built our house in Delhi some years ago, this was not by choice but compulsion. Anand Lok, where we live, has barely a hundred houses, no market and the gates remain closed most of the time. Yet even within this sanctuary, the city has a way of springing nasty surprises. A couple of years back, the house next door was pulled down to be replaced with a luxurious centrally air-conditioned edifice complete with jacuzzi and gymnasium. The owners, surprisingly, were not business people. The husband was a senior finance manager of a company and the wife a postgraduate in mathematics. They were not only softspoken and polite but even showed rare courtesy in Delhi by removing the debris after their house had been constructed. We could not help wondering how such nice people had so much money. Some months ago, our neighbours disappeared into thin air. Enquiries revealed that the man had been caught embezzling as much as a hundred million rupees from his company which had now seized all his assets including, of course, the house.

It is this unpredictability of life in Delhi that still makes me, after all these years, feel a stranger in the city.

Tyrannies at work

MADHU JAIN

WE moved home recently. I jokingly refer to our new-old home in Vasant Vihar as the final resting place, before the really final resting place. This is it: no more moves. For me it is a return to my parents' home, though they have long been gone. The last time I lived here was in 1991, the year my father passed away.

It feels like another country today. We have added a floor to my parents' sweetly modest bungalow. But it still seems all shrunken next to the huge apartment complexes that look like bonsai high-rises, all deformed and bulgy – stunted before they could really take flight. They are popping up all over the place as if the soil of the neighbourhood had overdosed on fertility drugs. These are the neither-here-nor-there type of structures that are a builder's dream and a neighbour's nightmare.

There is a reason for telling you all this. We are told in hushed tones about the Faustian deal with builders. We are told that some of these massive four-storied buildings have swimming pools on top. A few have terrace gardens. Now here comes the rub. That swimming pool in the sky hurts, a lot: there is an acute shortage of water in

Vasant Vihar. In the short spell that we have been here, four friends – and one relative – have asked us if they can wash their clothes in our washing machine. A couple even bathed here two mornings. Their taps have run dry; their bore wells have dried up. Nobody goes next door for a cup of sugar; they go for a glass of water. They say that the next time countries go to war, it won't be over oil; it will be over water.

I hope I am not digressing. This article is not about Vasant Vihar and large stretches of Delhi going the Fatehpur Sikri way, dried out, all life sucked out of them much before their time. It is about the continuing metamorphosis of this city, my city. Once half-condescendingly referred to as a fat village that thinks itself a city, Delhi has become a megalopolis, bursting at its seams.

Where there are all sorts of tyrannies at work.

The most obvious, and the most lethal, is the prevailing tyranny of might – what those ruddy builders have in the me-first, greed-is-good credo that's been the reigning *mantra* in this city for the past decade or so. According to this code you steal water, you steal electricity, you steal public land, you steal others' phone time. And it's not just the poor or the have-nots who are doing this. The rich and famous are. In fact, they are also stealing their neighbour's sleep and peace of mind with their gigantic generators.

But more about the city's soul and its tyrannies later.

Delhiwallahs number close to 14 million. Another million come in to work each day. And thousands more disgorge from buses and trains to seek a better life – just as they did a few decades ago into Bombay. During the last decade of the last century the population grew by 43%. This new Mecca of the country is growing outwards, gobbling up all the villages and land on its outskirts at such an alarming rate that it will soon take on the size and vital statistics of a country, a nation-city.

While the heart, the original core of the city that exists behind Delhi Gate, hangs on to some of the romance of the past and its history – even implodes – the rest of Delhi ostensibly marches towards modernity. Delhi and suburban Delhi grow futuristic. Little bits of America sprout on Indian soil: fabulous glass covered high-rises, new townships with what almost look like roll-on lawns, golf clubs, gyms, resorts, hotels, shopping malls, motels go on endlessly. Hold your nose and you could be in parts of New Jersey.

Many sport the not made-in-India look with names like Malibu, Palms, Charmwood – names out of Hollywood films. Some of the residential complexes look as if they have just landed, prefabricated, from other worlds, like UFOs. Advertizements for some of them actually boast that there is nothing Indian about them. Stores that sell only European furniture or readymade kitchens make sure that the interiors are as 'foreign' as the exteriors. Some of the furniture has seen no Indian wood. Some kitchens are even advertized as *bai*-proof: no Indianisms can creep in here.

Made in India and things ethnic are getting to be in bad odour. After all, the city has to match its Beautiful People: blonde streaks in the hair and blue or green contact lenses propel you up the beauty ladder faster these days. Twenty years behind the Mediterranean women, and 10 years behind the Dubai/Pakistani look. The old song needs a rewrite: *Beautiful, beautiful blue eyes; I'll never love brown eyes again*.

Our history books tell us about the many Delhis that have existed through time: we are supposed to be the eighth or ninth *avatar*. Our sociologists tell us about the many Delhis which exist simultaneously today: medieval India and 21st century India cheek-by-jowl. You have only to traipse through Hauz Khas village (our ersatz Greenwich village) or its clones like Lado Sarai and Mehrauli to experience this *jugalbandi* of different time zones. I will never forget the inauguration of Verandah, a huge shop beyond Mehrauli that houses – under one roof – the wares of the fanciest designers of interiors, furniture and garden ware.

It was an amazing sight: the Mercs and BMWs had to offload their precious living cargo a few hundred yards before the shop: there was a traffic jam with cursing bus drivers, truck drivers, tempos, and the rest of India, it seemed. So, those in their elegant finery, their fine *dupattas* or handkerchiefs held to their toffee noses had to hitch their sarees or skirts or pants and walk over (sweating, cursing) dung-laden stretches to get to the El Dorado of style. Where pate and smoked salmon, air kisses and the arbiters of taste awaited them. The locals looked as if they did not know what had hit them. *Yeh Mera* India?

Don't get me wrong. I loved it too, and also cursed my way there and back. It's just that these juxtapositions of opposing worlds that India, and most spectacularly Delhi, offers at every turn are so compelling. The first world and the third world keep invading each other's space. And often, they clash: the tragic death of Jessica Lall at Tamarind Court was a consequence of the clash of civilizations. Out beyond Qutub Minar, the border lines between rural and sophisticate/NRI/urban/with-it India are very fuzzy. Playboys of the eastern world, make that semi-rural world, with their guns and knives and pockets groaning with money made from the sale of their rural land are not very easy guests or gatecrashers. Their cosmopolitanism takes them only so far as the branded jeans they wear and the alcohol they guzzle. Their minds tick to medieval clocks.

Whose Delhi is it anyway?

With so many Delhis I begin to wonder: where is my Delhi? Where is the centre of Delhi? Perhaps, there is no longer any one centre to this city whose haphazard growth has spiralled beyond control, both upwards and outwards. Each area has its own shopping complexes, gathering places to swan about and be seen at, places to mark your presence on some invisible social register. Delhi has been rapidly transformed from a sleepy city of *babus* and diplomats (who used to be almost quarantined in their post-colonial versions of cantonments) to a wannabe international metropolis.

When I was growing up, and even until a few years ago, Connaught Circus was the centre of the universe for me. All roads led here. You went there to see your movies. You went there to eat. You went there to shop. You went there to buy your clothes, your books, your essentials and inessentials. You went there to flirt, to lock eyes with somebody you fancied. The Cottage Industries emporium was a Mecca of sorts, a daily pilgrimage. No matter where we lived, we made sure it was on the way home from the university.

Although I did my Masters in English Literature from Delhi University, I went to school and college in the United States. Thus, for me, CP was a place to capture a childhood and adolescence I never had in India. It was the reclamation of an imaginary past. Janpath was like the malls of Mussourie and Simla: you didn't exist unless you registered your presence here. Many crushes were born and died here. Or blossomed into love and marriage, or whatever. Connaught Place and Janpath were like one end of a compass. For wherever you went, and however far you went, you always came back. This part of the city gave you your bearings. Now it is just one of the many places.

While CP was for the coming-of-age days, Khan Market for me is always surrounded by a halo of nostalgia. It is in a sense childhood regained: I still search for that indefinable taste of the chocolate of Carryhom ice cream. I still crave for the sight and taste of the pungent black and white bulls-eye mints. No doubt there are better mints and better ice creams. But they don't come with a whiff of childhood wonder and excitement.

Khan Market was the centre of the universe of my childhood – before my family moved overseas. We always lived within walking or biking distance of it. Whether we were in Shan Nagar (now Bharati Nagar), Wellesley Road (now Zakir Hussain Marg) and finally Lodhi Garden, we made our daily pilgrimage to Khan Market for our fix of ice cream. It was a protected world. Delhi did not extend beyond this little world of privileged brats of bureaucrats.

Of course, there was school: the anachronism of red brick Convent of Jesus and Mary, with the man with a black tin trunk of goodies like chocolate fudge *barfi* and the most amazing *samosas* – the likes of which I have never had again. But that again was an oasis, despite some of the sadistic teachers and strict nuns, in a changing world. No other worlds existed: servant quarters were out of sight, out of mind. I only remember the few flutters when the *jamardarni* washed our clothes (my mother had no hang-ups and the word caste was not even in our vocabulary) and my *dadi* had fits.

Wait a minute, I am leaving something out. I must have been a terrible snob. My first memories of Delhi are when I returned, all of four, from London with my parents and we visited my maternal grandparents in Old Delhi, near the railway station and behind Novelty cinema. Their home was really two huge elephant garages – they must have been part of the stables of the Mughals. Dara Singh's in-laws lived next door. And I am forever being ribbed about turning up my nose at the 'broken houses' in India. If only I had my notebook out then: what a vibrant place, with its courtyards and courtyard politics with my grandmother, the general wise woman of the area. We used to cross the two worlds – from sanitized, bureaucratic Lutyens' Delhi to Shiv Ashram, as it was then called, in a little black Hillman. That world, too, has disappeared. Must be a shopping centre that has come up over the quaint little printing press and the open spaces where we played *gulli danda*.

Delhi is the magnet city, a Mecca for those looking for jobs. The new migrants are not the poor, the refugees of the past, or the *bhaiyas* and labourers coming in to fulfil the post Independence Nehruvian India. Or the stenos from the South whose fingers worked at supersonic speed in dictation and typing without whom the babus building a new India would collapse. More lately, it is the educated affluent from other parts of the country and the world who are flocking here. Especially the expats and NRIs.

As a journalist looking for more talking heads on various subjects, one often trekked out to Bombay, or called upon the eggheads of Calcutta or Bangalore for insights into what was happening in India and elsewhere. Today, most of them are in Delhi. The intelligentsia for what it's worth: artists, writers, sociologists, shrinks, whatever, are here to stay. You don't have to go to them.

Meanwhile, back to the many tyrannies of the city.

There's the tyranny of the rupee-dollar. Many among the privileged have seceded from the rest – into their private oases. With private couriers, security, water, electricity, communication – mobiles and the Internet, even private airplanes, they don't need the government or public sector to service them. Look, honey, I shrunk the state.

There is the tyranny of beauty. The ugly and the fat are becoming invisible. Nonentities. Indian women are notching up crowns the way American athletes harvest gold medals at the Olympics. Beauty has become currency. Little misses are being pushed by their parents in small town India to enter beauty contests and hoist their families up social and economic ladders. Both men and women spend hours and small fortunes in beauty parlours and gyms to hang on to youth.

Adonis is an everywhere-man now. Today, if you don't look good, it's your fault. Corporate ladders become less slippery if you are well groomed. Beauty has also become big business, with mushrooming neighbourhood parlours and multinationals flooding the market with cosmetics and hair dyes. Ambitious moms drag their daughters, often as young as eight, to beauty parlours to get the hair on their arms and faces removed. Beauty is also power. The body has become a temple. And not just with the young. Nobody wants to grow old. You fight age with all you've got: cosmetics, cosmetic surgery, vitamins, protein shakes, gyms or new age religion for the next best thing on offer: inner beauty.

You can play god with yourself: don't like the bulbous tummy, get a liposuction, don't like the downward droop of the mouth or long nose, get it fixed. It's the time for reinventing yourself, casting yourself in the image of your ideal.

There is the tyranny of the uncouth, those who can talk the loudest. And post-Kargil, post-Gujarat, post- a lot of unfortunate things, there is complete polarization in the drawing rooms of Delhi. Alas, the flip side of modernization is turning out to be fundamentalism. Nobody holds their fires at dinner parties. Political correctness is a thing of a more genteel past.

There's the tyranny of the nouveaus: patronage has long shifted hands to the contractors and the inhabitants of page three and page six. With it, the death of Bohemia – a way of life ends up like a restaurant décor and artists have become five-star accessories. Invited for the occasion, to lend some ambience, like some *bandar ka naach*.

There's the tyranny of sexuality worn on the sleeve. In-your-face women's sexuality is ubiquitous – on ramps, little screens, big screens, clubs, music videos and the street. Himbos with Popeye muscles strut down ramps and preen narcissistically from the glossies and the big screens – the new objects of desire, as beefcake becomes cheesecake.

In this city on the move, looking good is an imperative: gyms, beauty parlours, health food shops, nutritionists, slimming parlours, fashion schools, grooming schools, dancing schools proliferate, like *paanwalas*.

The new motto in this world is: if you have it, flash it. So people who may have once put away their jewels and heirlooms now let it all hang out, no more nods to socialism. It's not just the Beautiful People who flash clothes, jewels and lifestyles. Real people do too. No longer is there any real distinction between new money and old money – it is just money, neat. It's the best leveller. It no longer takes generations to arrive. The PTP route is the fastest.

The tyranny of the spiritual gurus. An age of instant gratification also calls for Instant Nirvana. New Age spirituality is the reigning rage. The mind bazaar is open overtime – and the cash registers are ringing ceaselessly. New Age Gurus and spiritual boutiques and books and Reiki centres in garages are mushrooming in cities. Life according to Vaastu, Feng Shui and your personal guru, like your personal trainer. The spiritual kitty party has also arrived – gossip is being replaced by new age babble.

I could go on with the tyrannies and the perfidies of Delhi. But ask me to move. No way. This is home. I just have to get myself a new compass.

Adab nama

RENUKA NARAYANAN

MANY travellers have described Delhi, from Ibn Batuta and Nicolao Manucci to Emily Eden. Today, sociologists, historians and journalists may well echo Shahjahan's engraving in the Red Fort that Delhi is heaven on earth, for there's so much to study and write about. For a single woman who's lived out several phases of her life in this hot and dusty plain, it is a landscape made luminous with love, adventure, sorrow and soul-growth. This city hugs you close but like Mowgli in the jungle, you have to know the passwords to its favour. Like any great metropolis, Delhi has its own, which the impatient, the scornful and the disbelieving are unlikely to discover because Delhi has so much bad press as a louche, uncouth sort of place.

To the wondering eye, however, certain cultural clues to handling Delhi 'situations' become apparent with close observation:

The standoff: Most commonly experienced in traffic jams. Neither side will give way and prefers to stay locked eyeball-to-eyeball in time-wasting macho bristle. It is considered unmanly in Delhi to back off. So don't attempt to match them in this incurable display of testosterone as a lifestyle. Throw up your hands, laugh, and say,

Jaane bhi do, guru if you're male. Or else, *Arre bhaiyya, jaana bhi do, na*! if female (in dulcet tones, for aggressive females seem to upset Delhi men very deeply, whereas in Mumbai the men are obviously used to being bully-bounced). Watch them back off at once – they haven't lost 'face' since *you* made the first conciliatory move. They'd rather be moving too, but centuries of conditioning keeps them riveted to the road in stony silence. They're very thankful really that you flapped a flag first! In realpolitik, it is this attitude that noticeably characterizes Indo-Pak relations.

The verbal slap: Ever watched a Delhiite blow up somebody for sloppy work, like a plumber, carpenter, sub-editor, management trainee or clerk? The trick, which no other place but the Punjab has mastered, is to scold first, but carry on in a normal tone afterwards. Displeasure is communicated clearly but dialogue is not cut off, because work must go on. The offender is not allowed time and space to brood, but put back on the conveyor belt after being hauled out for a good slap. Note this, it is a masterly method of keeping life moving.

The flourish: Gestures mean a lot in Delhi. *Kanjoos* South Indians and Maharashtrians have a lot to learn in this department. (Bengalis are better socialized and enjoy food enormously, so they adapt best to this local custom). An office friend's birthday means a treat and a present. It might mean flowers on the table before the felicitee trickles in to work. Likewise, a colleague's departure signals an office party or lunch at some 'nice' place. Everyone must share willingly in this social spending. It is considered deplorable form to grumble or evade participation in such revels.

Kaam chori: One of the most annoying things about Delhi is its lack of 'professionalism'. The most elementary chores get done only with the diplomacy and persuasive exertions of a Metternich or a Kissinger. And yet, charm we never so wisely, the jibbing travel agent, *sarkari babu*, gardener, electrician or maid will only oblige with the tacit promise of *baksheesh*. You mustn't blame the people of Delhi. Save the Punjab, which A, has a work culture and B, is proud of it, or a few conscientious states of the Northeast, most of India is lazy beyond belief. Blame both nurture and nature. The rivers deposit rich silt on the banks. Food almost grows itself in the fertile Gangetic plain. Rulers of every nationality and persuasion left you alone as long as you paid tax. Delhi seems to echo the popular medieval saying of the northern wheat fields: *Khata peeta laahe da/Rehnda Ahmed Shahe da*. This cynical worldview is not to be wondered at in the peasant-turned-citizen who eats, drinks and makes merry with this season's harvest, because who knows which new ruler will be suzerain next year (or, in a democracy, after five years)? Besides, the weather is either too hot or too humid most of the year. QED: why exert oneself unnecessarily, unless there's a chance of a little profit? (Mumbaikars are praised a lot in this department, but it's not that they're better, it's because geography is history. They spend their lives going up and going down on a narrow strip between North and South Mumbai. So there's nowhere to dodge, no nice parks to go play cards in, snooze or throw orange peel and peanut shells, like in Delhi).

Chor-police: To Delhi's young, this term connotes a game with thieves and law-enforcers on opposing sides. As youth ripens into worldly wisdom, 'chor-police' reveals its true meaning. Both are the same. The Indian Penal Code was instituted by the British as a means of keeping 'the natives' under control and not amended much after independence. The police are thus still seen as oppressors and not friends of the people – except, of course, at a price. Honest cops are tiny atolls in a great ocean of police corruption and venality. The rules are suspicious of one's motives and discourage involvement with one's fellow-beings. So the citizens of Delhi tend to fend for themselves and rarely extend a helping hand to accident victims. In alleged tinderboxes like the Walled City, the atmosphere is more loving and intense between Hindus and Muslims than between Hindu and Hindu in fashionable areas like South Delhi. The police in fact say that the future riot-prone area is not the walled city but North East Delhi where vast slum colonies have taken root.

Socio-civic hiccups: When the rules don't treat citizens as grown-up, responsible people, it perpetuates lack of civic responsibility. Garbage is dumped outside without thought of the dirt and disease it causes, let alone lack of aesthetics. Cars are parked selfishly without consideration for other users. Most noticeably, there is callousness on the part of the affluent towards the have-nots, who naturally froth with rage at the disparity in lifestyles. To protect himself from the fury of the poor, the intelligent Delhiite avoids any show of conspicuous consumption. This means outward discretion in what he drives, wears and throws away.

As a teenager swimming at the Golf Club pool, it was early trauma, ordering an innocent club sandwich after a swim and being hissed at by the bearer (no grown-up was around), that it was the equivalent of one month's rations. But equally, when affection and politeness set the tone of a relationship, a maid will gift her mistress a silver bangle or a pretty bunch of flowers on her birthday! The *ayah* who is secure, respected and happy will insist on treating her small charge to ice cream and stay on as a faithful family retainer for years, even when the *babalog* are grown up – despite the blandishments of other *memsahibs* who offer more.

The 'heppyburday': It is the fashion for parents of young children in Delhi to advertize their joy to the world with the rite of passage called the *Burdaypaati*. The occasion itself may be phonetically inscribed as the Heppyburday. If the cold season, the burdaypaati is held in a local park. Urchins gather hopefully at the fringes while plump young people cavort amidst swings and seesaws in their festive best, each with an *adivasi* attendant from Chhota Nagpur, Ranchi or if you enquire further, Jashpur. (Many citizens however believe that such ayahs are hatched mysteriously aged 15-plus in a yellow procurement house near the petrol pump at South Extension Part I, and not the most strenuous attempts to make them see the map will convince them that it is otherwise).

Towards the fateful moment of 'cake-cutting', the mothers and fathers of the invited guests usually make their appearance. This nice piece of timing is not merely to ensure their share of the birthday tea but to critically inspect the quality of the 'back-gift'. While the naïve may consider such excessive concern with the return gift foolish, in truth, it is the Delhiite's early teaching ground for social responsibility in the all-important business of 'Keeping Face' through future birthdays, *naamkarans* and weddings when the children grow up. The importance of return gifts is indicated as far back as in classical epics like the Mahabharata and the Ramayana. The Sanskrit term for it is *maryada*. (Latin societies are known to cherish similar customs, but for reasons not clear to us in India, nobody seems to study them with quite that level of curiosity and judgement as the good people of, say, Heidelberg, study our tribal customs. Perhaps it is simply that the colonial gaze has never blinked or wavered, but just renamed itself the neo-colonial gaze?).

Public events: The tax-paying citizens of Delhi have a long track record of keeping quiet while every kind of authoritarian display or atrocity is paraded under their nose. In Aurangzeb's time (late 17th century), they watched, sighing and keening, as their favourite prince Dara Shikoh was paraded in chains on an elephant en route to arrest and beheading. Not much later, they gathered in Chandni Chowk to watch Guru Tegh Bahadur's execution. Only a low caste sweeper, Jaita Rangreta, had the cojones to rescue the Guru's corpse from further indignity.

They flocked mumchance again to watch when George V arrived for the Delhi Durbar in the winter of 1911, Lord Curzon, the then Viceroy, had Kingsway Camp built in record speed beyond Outram Line to the north of Delhi. Afterwards a mini Cleopatra's Needle marked the spot where the royal tent was pitched. In florid Persian royalese borrowed wholesale from the displaced Mughals, the Urdu plaque reveals that George (Ala-e-Hazrat) announced the news of his coronation earlier that year in England to the assembled kings and nobility who had gathered there in his *khidmat* (service).

After having only these shameful frolics to watch, imagine the joy of the citizens when Republic Day parades began to be held on balmy January mornings, while everywhere the free flag tossed above their heads. The city came together again during the Emergency, when urchins went around with Congress handbills that they were hired to distribute, and as they accosted each passer-by, they smiled beseechingly and whispered, 'But please vote for the Janata Party.' Afterwards, when Mrs. Gandhi lost the polls, there was dancing in the streets and many drums. Equally, the city rejoiced when the country brought her back again.

Alas, these profound pleasures were spoilt forever after 1982, when Punjab terrorism began to spoil everyday life in Delhi. The city's new lease of pride in its democratic maturity which reflected the whole country's, was destroyed forever in 1984 after Mrs. Gandhi's assassination, when the anti-Sikh riots made gutters run red. Is it atonement that makes Hindus flock outside Gurdwara Shish Ganj in Chandni Chowk that marks Guru Tegh Bahadur's martyrdom and drink the water of floor-washings flowing off the pavement as *charanamrit*? (It was certainly one of Delhi's most festive seasons when the Khalsa celebrated its 300th anniversary in 1999: almost every vehicle on the road sported saffron pennants with the Sikh emblem).

Delhi burned again during the Mandal riots when young men set first buses and then themselves, ablaze. It was a Black Diwali in 1989, when gangs of youth went from door to door, to ask the people not to celebrate in protest against V.P. Singh's policies. And in the dead of winter, some months later, when V.P. Singh lost his support in the Lok Sabha at around midnight, Delhi was watching intently on TV. The minute Singh's defeat was announced, the air resounded with firecrackers hoarded since Black Diwali for just this moment.

Delhi does remember it's a city every now and then. The trouble perhaps is that so much blood has soaked into Delhi's soil, that extremes of violence and apathy prevail. The passport to Delhi's dislike is actually simple: raise onion prices, hike bus fares and threaten to diminish the only sector with job security. (In other words, a *sarkari* workplace where extra money may be made and work hours profitably spent in some nice park, with orange peel and peanut shells mounding up around).

The cocktail party: When the Page Three People party, there are several predictable behaviour patterns among Delhiites, also observed in Mumbai or Bangalore. Air kissing is fast and furious between people known to be sworn enemies. Business ladies of an ancient though not always honourable profession and handsome young men of similar business practices tend to discreetly pass delicately coloured (and sometimes scented) business cards around. The beauty of the cocktail is its democracy. A-lists and Z-lists mingle freely and every new configuration is a photo-op for the three-and-a-half lensmen always found at these events. It is as vibrant a picture of a functioning anarchy as any director of an institute of South Asian Studies could approve of and no less fascinating than Samoan islanders must have seemed to Margaret Meade.

The prayer meeting: Delhiites are perhaps the most dignified when it comes to death ceremonies. All their aggression is left at the door with their footwear at the gurdwara or ashram hall. They file in quietly, sit in orderly rows, clad in sombre white and weep noiselessly into well-ironed hankies. Their exuberance and sense of fun, their enormous, lusty appetites for food, drink, dance and display seem to belong to people from another planet. The music of the *shabad* or *bhajan* is soothing and understated. When the last song has been sung, a *sevadar* hands out *prasad* neatly while a white-covered table holds sealed glasses of mineral water. The family of the bereaved line up at the door and those who came to the ceremony trickle past them quietly with a *namaste*. There is a grace and order befitting the finality of the occasion that cannot fail to move any bystander. Of course, the minute they leave and join the roaring rivers of traffic they switch emotional gears and go right back to being their aggressive, bonhomous selves. But to know them is to love them: their *savoir vivre* is a celebration of life!

Of people and places

JASLEEN DHAMIJA

LIVING in Delhi has been for me a rich experience and despite all its drawbacks, I have come to love this city. Even today I love it as one can only love an impossible lover.

I see Delhi as a microcosm of greater India, for I can experience all the different cultures in my own locality, the MIG apartments at Saket. As I walk my dog I see *rangoli* from South India and hear the strains of nadaswaram floating down the road. On festive days there is the Bengali *alpana* and voices singing Rabindra sangeet. The call of the *azan* is heard every day. On Guru Nanak's birthday one is unceremoniously woken by firecrackers and *prabhat pheri* at the crack of dawn. I curse this religiosity, but a part of me is happy that old traditions survive. On Diwali all the houses are lit, with twinkling oil lamps, candles and the new, tiny electric lights. My heart fills with joy as I share in the joyful celebration of the festival. Holi involves visits to neighbours, with *thalis* full of *gulal* and sweets. We converge at a neighbour's to sing the rather risqué songs, imbibing the *kanji* and *pakoris* made by the Kayasth women, and the stronger brew made by the men.

I came from a small mountain town, Abbotabad, in the North Western Frontier Province, which nestled in a cup-shaped valley surrounded by mountains. From my bedroom we could see the snow-clad mountains. In winter when it snowed the school closed and we would play in the snow. It was in 1940 that I was suddenly transported to this big town, Delhi. I saw my first telephone. We had the old fashioned standing telephone with a trumpet shaped earphone and I shrank back everytime I heard the disembodied voice echoing in my ear. There were the big red public buses known as Gwalior Transport, which frightened me. I saw my first peacock, proud and beautiful. It had flown across the road from the Ridge on to our terrace leaving me enchanted. Till then I had only seen it on my mother's jewellery.

We lived in Civil Lines, at Khyber Pass, in an old family house built during the time of the Raj when the Old Secretariat was the seat of the colonial government. Across from the house was the Ridge, with the flag staff, the scene of the simian Altu Faltu's romance. Mall Road was towards its right and Rajpur Road to its left, running parallel to the Ridge. Beyond was the Old Secretariat, the terminal for Bus No.9, which travelled from the New Secretariat and carried many of the lovers of Delhi University.

The Ridge had equestrian paths where the English rode their horses and we went for our evening walks. I often took my dog, a dachshund, for walks on Rajpur Road, where Biren De, the painter lived. He referred to me as 'the long sentence with a semicolon at the end of it.'

We would travel by bus to New Delhi to visit my uncle who lived on Hailey Road. The journey was always exciting. One went past the fashionable Maidens Hotel, under Kashmiri Gate and then the upmarket Ritz cinema which showed English movies. When we returned home at night, the bus passed through G.B. Road, the red light district, invariably lit up with throngs of dressed up women standing on the terraces and calling out to the men below. Mother would tell me not to look up but I usually sneaked a peek at the scene, wondering what those strangely dressed women were doing under so many lamps.

Our neighbour was the Registrar at Delhi University and he had a plump little wife. They had no children and no one came to visit them. In the evenings we heard mellifluous music coming from their house and I heard the elders whisper that he had married a singing girl, deserting his family and grown up children. No one mixed with them. Once when we met on the stairs she smiled and asked me to come over. She would dress me up in beautiful clothes, sing to me and I danced for her. She gave me chocolates and cooked delicacies. We had a wonderful time until my father spotted me all dressed up one day and I was forbidden to go to their house any more.

School was Presentation Convent near the old railway station and run by Irish nuns. Girls from old Kayasth families attended the school, as did Muslim girls from the old city. They came in *purdah* cars, but once in the purdah was abandoned and we were all the same – playing together, studying, sharing our tiffin and giggling over silly jokes. The school had an English and an Indian section. In my second year at school I was transferred to the English section. I wept, refused to go to school and made my father request my transfer back to the Indian section. The Mother Superior scolded my father and told him how absurd his request was, for every parent was asking for his or her child to be transferred to the English section. It was not for my academic brilliance, but because of my light skin that I was given this privilege.

The year 1942 saw the Quit India movement and my brother, who was at Hindu College and enthused by the freedom struggle, suggested that I write 'Quit India' on the school blackboard on the day we were expecting the Vicerine. He, of course, practised writing 'Quit India' on our back stairs, little realizing that it was used only by the sweeper when he came to clean the lavatories.

Our second home in Delhi was No.8 Hailey Road, where my uncle lived. Next door lived the dashingly handsome pilot, Biju Patnaik. From the windows we would watch figures flitting in and out of their kitchen and sometimes into uncle's house. I heard my brother whisper, 'That is Aruna Asaf Ali'. Sometimes, there were other minor leaders of the freedom struggle, who were all underground.

I still remember the picnics on Vasant Panchami. The most memorable were the big family picnics at Okhla, occasions when young men met the girls and the elders flew kites. We all played *kolrda chipaki* and the boys got the opportunity to talk to girls, to fleetingly hold a hand or the end of a *dupatta*. It was at one of these picnics that my brother-in-law saw my sister and fell in love with her. *Pitaji* reluctantly agreed though he felt 'they are business people,' who were frowned upon. Our families preferred grooms from professional backgrounds, though they did not mind brides from business families as they brought good dowries.

One year we went in a *tonga* for a picnic all the way to the Qutub. The journey took us nearly two hours. Father promised to take us for the *Phul-walo-ki-Sair* in Mehrauli at the culmination of the tonga race, run from the walled city to Mehrauli. We never were able to make it, but I listened avidly to descriptions of the young Muslim men with their decorated tongas and *ikkas*, racing down the road. Mehrauli decorated itself to receive them. Then came the procession of the local elite and Delhi society going to the shrine of Pir Kaki to offer flower fans created by the flower merchants. There were also groups of *qawwali* singers, who sang at the *mazar*.

Connaught Place, which had large restaurants with dance floors, was the most fashionable shopping centre. I remember going for tea into Wengers and sitting at the tables by the side of the dance floor to watch the English and American soldiers dance with the Anglo-Indian girls. We had tea and chocolate pastries, but my heart was fixated at the sight of the dancing couples. I remember romanticizing that I was one of the girls dancing in the arms of a tall white mustachioed man, instead of with a girl, as we did during school socials.

Those were the days of innocence, when our pleasures were simple: celebrations of festivals, family picnics, and weddings when we got new clothes. On Sundays, school friends came over and we walked to the Jamuna. Every summer we bought large watermelons for one rupee, which we floated down the river, chasing them into the shallows and then eating them with great gusto. A few rupees were all that the picnic cost. Our friendships were based on shared interests without awareness of caste, creed or status. We celebrated all the festivals together. At Eid we looked forward to the *kebabs* and the *biryani*; at Christmas to Santa Claus and the plum pudding. All our friends came to us for Gurpurab and Baisakhi and we trooped off with thousands of pilgrims to celebrate at Majnu-ka-Tilla and join the devotees to offer *sewa* at the free kitchen, to roll out the *chapatis* and sit in a line together with the others to share in the *langar* of *dal*, *subzi*, *kachumbar* and *roti*.

Then came independence. I remember going with my father to Parliament House to listen to a debate on the national flag. I was thrilled to see Jawaharlal Nehru, who had visited our ancestral home in Abbotabad, as he had been at the University in England with Vade Chachaji. We visited Mahatma Gandhi at Birla House and I was so proud that he recognized my sister, who had sung for him every day for over a month when Gandhiji stayed with us at Abbotabad.

Independence was marred by the partition of the country. Relatives from Lahore, Rawalpindi, Abbotabad poured in with the few belongings they had salvaged. There was fear in their eyes and despair on their faces. Alongside the horror were the uplifting stories of Muslim friends, who had risked their own lives to save their neighbours. We were fortunate not to lose any relatives. They however, lost everything.

Our home became a dormitory. Beds were spread on the floor and people sat in shifts to eat their meals. There was a threat to us from a nearby Press where a large number of people had gathered, fleeing the killing and looting in the old city. From our terrace we saw fires burning all around us. We heard threatening voices shouting *Har Har Mahadev, Bole So Nihal*, and *Allah Hu Akbar*. I witnessed the senseless stabbing of a young boy on the road in front of our house. I knew fear and it took me years to get over my paranoia of any religious celebration. We were witness to the sad sight of a large group of Meo families marching with their cattle. They looked fierce and the streets emptied. We watched them from behind barred doors, tall and handsome, walking firm and proud towards Pakistan, their meagre belongings balanced on their animals. They were our people and it was sad to see them go.

When school reopened, my Muslim friends were no longer there. They never came back. The telephones went unanswered and I wept for my beautiful friend Nasreen, who was lost to me.

Our many guests found temporary places. Some hoped that this was a crazy period and they would go back. Others knew better and began to rebuild their lives in an unknown territory. Slowly life came back to normal. But echoes of the tragedy were felt when father would meet people, his old accountant for example, who had lost all members of his family. Or an old acquaintance from Lahore, who had been a rich man and was now back to where he started, a *kabariwala*. A mother came begging, pleading with father to intervene with her husband to take back their young daughter who had been recovered from Pakistan. For my parents' generation, separation from their homeland was a great loss. Even today you hear, from those who are still around, how everything in Abbotabad was the best. The water was sweet, the fruit was the juiciest, people were wonderful and the air clean, pure and healthy. My grandmother whose name was Tooti, 'lady parrot', would sigh and say *'Bhardea Abbotabada kadi bhulda nahi.'* Wicked Abbotabad, I cannot forget you.

In 1949 I joined Miranda House, the new college on the Delhi University campus. We were the hip girl students and our batch had Sagari Chengappa, who was the heartthrob of the university. Natwar Singh, the ace debator of St. Stephen's College, was forever offering his non-existent kingdom for her. Sagari played hostess for her uncle, General Cariappa, and would sneak in goodies for us when she returned to the hostel. Madhur Bahadur, later Jaffrey of Merchant Ivory films and the wonderful cookbooks, known even then as a consummate actress, was wooed by Saeed Jaffrey. There was Sujatha Mathai, petite and beautiful, who became a well-known poet, the Saraswat Brahmin beauty Sunanda Surkund, who attracted a lot of attention. Among the seniors there was the oomphy Uma Vasudev and Malati Bhatia, the attractive tennis player. Bright Indu Chatterjee, who married and went away to Pakistan. Romila Thapar, who even then stood head and shoulders above everyone and of course the unforgettable Sheila Bahadur, with her brilliance, beautiful voice and witty conversation.

Our teachers too were characters. The neurotic principal Mrs. Thakurdas, Kamala Acheya with her face painted like a Kathakali mask who later married Professor V.K.R.V. Rao. There was Krishna Essuloff, who was always voluptuously wrapped in brilliant Kanjeevrams and of course the two friends Kapila Mallick (Vatsyayan) and Sita Chari, who tried to enlighten their callow students about English literature. There were college romances and scandals. Kadambari Viswanathan eloped with Krishan Rasgotra of External Affairs, old enough to be her father. There was my romance with the revolutionary Santosh Chatterjee and Asha Atal's with Harish Chandra, the Communist student leader. There was the delightful Shaila Umbegaonkar, who drove around in a mini Fiat which always had to be pushed up a slope, who ran off with her best friend Jayshree's boyfriend, the maverick Tilak Nijowne. He was supposedly brilliant, but never managed to get through his BA.

Delhi University was a hotbed of student politics, romance, scandal and intrigue. It was here that we acquired our skills for the big world. It was while looking after the leftist relief committee for students that I honed my organizational skills and later, as president of Miranda House, helped organize events.

Delhi was slowly losing the refinement of the old inhabitants. Punjabi entrepreneurship was burgeoning and a new way of life emerging. Food habits were changing. Fruit shops were coming up. The sweet shops, which originally sold their goods in mud pots and palm leaf baskets and banana leaves, were now selling them in cardboard boxes similar to western style pastry shops. The new restaurants and *dhabas* served in metal *thalis* or ceramic plates instead of the disposable *pattal*, leaf plates and cups. Bottled drinks began to be sold and fruit juice stalls, as well as egg and meat shops, sprouted in all the neighbourhoods. In some localities which had a lot of refugees, the *tandoor* became an integral part of the local scene. Women would send dough made into round balls and for two *annas* or one eighth of a rupee, ten chapatis would be made. For another two annas you could get a bowl of cooked dal. For many homes that was a meal in itself, accompanied by raw onions and some pickle.

Eating places came up and Moti Mahal, the true Indian restaurant, opened in Darya Ganj, the dividing line between Old and New Delhi. It served *tandoori* chicken, *makhani dal* and *nan*. The *nouveau riche* Punjabis came in their cars to feast. The restaurant added floors, bought up next door houses and transformed itself into an open-air restaurant creating new genre of Indo-European eatery. Here the emphasis was not on ambience, but on food, and the newly emerging middle class felt more at ease. The Pathan waiters with their starched white salwars and shirts, large upturned moustaches and kohl in their eyes, greeted customers heartily with folded hands, with *jiyo ji, bhapi ji, sat bachan ji*, as they placed generous bowls of pickled onions to be munched while waiting for the crisply done tandoori chicken.

The pre-partition Punjabi families, mostly Sikhs, part of the construction mafia that built New Delhi and who had made it rich, were very much part of the richie-rich scene. Gossip had it that five of them colluded together, not allowing others to bid for the contracts as they shared the pickings. Others who sub-contracted from the big five or were related also made their millions; one started a furniture shop in Connaught Place and later the Coca Cola agency. Another, who had earlier been a clerk at Clarks Simla, rented a part of the Imperial hotel, subsequently bought the Maidens Hotel and then went on to start the Oberoi chain of hotels. They also helped a number of their relatives who came from West Punjab and absorbed them into their business or helped set them up. Some Punjabis, who had been part of the army, the Imperial Civil Service, had a base in Delhi and constituted the elite in Delhi Punjabi society.

They began storming the colonial bastions, the Imperial Gymkhana Club, the Golf Club, while others regularly went to the

Chelmsford Club, which had been set up by the Indians on the lines of the imperial clubs. Chelmsford club was very similar to Gymkhana, but a little showy. They began to Indianize by adding tables for rummy and introducing qawwalis on special occasions and tambola, which was more a part of the Anglo-Indian club culture during the colonial times.

In Connaught Place the Indian Coffee House was a hangout for unemployed intellectuals, journalists and insurance agents. There were family cabins where the girls sat with their men friends, whereas in the main hall the men sat the entire morning over a single cup of coffee. Every Sunday my friend Sunanda Surkund and I used to take the No. 9 bus from the Old Secretariat to Connaught Place and join the very popular family cabin, where Trevi Sen, the universal aunty, reigned supreme and a number of lively young men, Som Benegal, Richard Bartholomew, the poet and art critic, Baij Nath Malan, the intellectual bureaucrat and many others would join us. Trevi's naughty sense of humour, scintillating conversation and warm generosity, as well as the bevy of young girls around her, attracted all the young men. A number of romances budded in the Indian Coffee House.

The Constitution House, a set of barracks, was another meeting place in the '50s and '60s. It was later demolished and the External Ministry's hostel built in its place. It was a residence for artists, writers, bachelors and single women, who lived their own lives fully. The eccentric Vijay Tunga, writer and poet, carried on a battle with his waspish next door neighbour by speaking loudly to the wall. Suff and Elizabeth Brunner, the Hungarian mother and daughter painters, lived out their own fantasies under the patronage of Nehru. Satish Gujral and his beautiful wife, Kiran, started their romantic life and he began his portrait of Nehru and later Mrs. Gandhi, while residing there.

The government drumboy and photographer, Ram Dhamija, his neighbour, carried on his love affair with the extraordinary Mme Simki, Uday Shankar's partner. Ram Dhamija won me over by inviting me to private recitals of Balasaraswathy and the Dagar brothers at his stark bachelor digs. To see Bala imitate other dancers or interpret her favourite *padams* was for me a revelation. Mira Mallick, the brilliant young Indian Foreign Office debutante, had a host of admirers, who, one heard, fought over her. Nilima Sanyal, the sexy announcer at All India Radio, held court here and had a pick of admirers from all walks of life.

In the late '50s and mid '60s three personalities dominated the official, cultural and intellectual scene. There was Indira Gandhi, Nehru's hostess with her own coterie – Romesh and Raj Thapar, Inder Gujral, the leftist student leader from Lahore, the Bachchans and others, who discussed Oscar Wilde at the dinner table. There was Kamaladevi Chattopadhyaya with her large circle of political friends, young acolytes L.C. Jain, Raj Krishna, Som Benegal, as well as a number of friends from abroad, who came to visit her. She was committed to nurturing the living cultural traditions and was deeply involved with classical dance, the performing arts, theatre and crafts. She ran an open house for artists. Many of us worked with her in the movement for revival of craft traditions. Octavio Paz, the Mexican ambassador, was a frequent visitor to her house.

On the other hand there was Pupul Jayakar, a devotee of Krishnamurti. She had her own acolytes who listened avidly to her rather precious, intense conversations. She looked after the Handloom Board and appointed well-known artists to run the weaver service centres. Later, as head of Handicrafts Handloom Export Corporation and cultural advisor to Indira Gandhi, she organized the Festivals of India, letting loose on the world a dazzling display of arts, crafts, performing artists and snake charmers alongside minor royalty, who charmed the foreign public at a huge cost to the exchequer. The only person, who ever took her on was Mala Singh; she once did an extraordinary take off on her in her presence.

Sir Shankar Lal, a true representative of old Delhi family with his fondness for poetry, *mushaira* and nurturing Delhi's cultural life, encouraged the two *bahus* of the family, Sumitra Charat Ram and Sheila Bharat Ram to participate in Delhi's cultural scene. They set up two rival organizations. Bharatiya Kala Kendra, Sumitra's organization, enticed the Dagar brothers to Delhi and dhrupad came into its own. They organized ballets with Birju Maharaj and Kumudani Lakhia as the dancers and the Dagars providing the music. The Punjabi theatre of IPTA fame with Sheila Bhatia and Sneh Sanyal gave us the Punjabi opera, *Heer Ranjha*. Delhi was slowly emerging as a cultural centre.

The new all-knowing soothsayers during the '60s were the senior journalists. They had their own coteries. Sham Lal, the great intellectual, edited *The Times of India* and wrote his reviews as personal open letters. Girilal Jain worked with him and agreed with all that he said, until he took over from Sham Lal. There was Romesh Thapar of *Seminar* with his booming voice, his massive presence and his bright wife. They were all part of the armchair leftist group. Then there was Frank Moraes with his American friend Marilyn Silverstone, a brilliant photographer. Together with the young impetuous Nandan Kagal, they formed another group, which was very much part of the establishment. Nandan, of course, flitted from one group to another. Mulgaonkar of the *Hindustan Times* with his young attractive wife, Krishna Kaul and Mankekar of PTI and later *The Times of India*, were the other pillars of the print world. They all prophesied doom and doled out free advice to the government falling just short of advising God. Ajit Bhattacharjea belonged to everyone and no one, and took the Presidential protocol office to task for seating him at the bottom of the table with other journalists.

On the eve of my departure for Iran, Nandan Kagal organized a goodbye dinner with Sham Lal, the Thapars, Girlal Jain and R.K. Laxman, who was visiting from Bombay. Halfway through the evening they all got entangled in a heated discussion on the current situation in India. R.K. Laxman said to me, 'You see, Jasleen, they are not Indians. They are the new Olympians sitting at the Khyber Pass, condemning all that is happening in the Gangetic plain.'

Till the '70s, New Delhi remained a quiet capital town dominated by the civil servants. Bombay and Calcutta were the hubs of the commercial world and far more cosmopolitan. By the end of the decade, India began to open up to outside stimuli, influence peddling became a way of life and the presence of black money began to dominate all spheres. Business houses began to shift their offices nearer the corridors of power. PRO men and women and power brokers began mushrooming everywhere. The cocktail circuit became an important part of Delhi life, with politicians hobnobbing with government officials, diplomats and heads of the corporate world. Gone were the days when government officials had to get permission to attend a party thrown by an embassy or a business house with which their departments had dealings. The NRIs, with their foreign exchange, for which we were all starved, began peddling their influence. Delhi lost its innocence. It took on the appearance of a gaudy woman who lived to the hilt at all costs.

There were a few exceptions, among them the jovial, cigar smoking and encyclopedic Krishna Chaitanya, who refused to use the official car, except strictly on official business. He rode his motorcycle all over Delhi attending concerts, art exhibitions and plays. He was a prolific writer and wrote many books and reviewed art exhibitions as well as Indian and western music concerts.

Delhi attracted all the talented artists and the elite flocked to the theatre, music concerts and art galleries to flaunt their jewellery and designer clothes. A new class came up – young affluent kids, the children of businessmen and senior civil servants, with plenty of money to throw around at discos, five star hotels and cultural events. Standing apart were the *jhola walas*, who frowned on this hedonist lifestyle and became the conscience keepers of the society. They set up NGOs, held study circles and countered in a small way the carefree lifestyle of the *nouveau riche*. The jhola walas mingled with the jetset at the art and culture happenings and often enjoyed the good things of life with great condescension.

However, the cultural life of Delhi flowered. The season from October to March offered a rich selection of dance, music, theatre, art shows, installations, events and happenings. There were coteries, which surrounded the cultural gurus. Gita Kapur and Vivan Sundaram had their favourite artists who they promoted unrelentingly. Alkazi through Art Heritage Gallery did so in a subtler manner, even as Manjeet Bawa helped Renu Modi to develop her stable of artists at Espace Gallery, whom she marketed through her Marwari and corporate contacts. Chandralekha, Dashrath Patel and Sadanand Menon dominated the dance scene, and were soon challenged by the classicist, Sonal Mansingh, who fought her lonely battles.

The grand dirty old man, Khushwant Singh, maintained his image of a sharp tongue and a robust libidinous sense of humour, successfully hiding the serious man whose best work is on the *gurbani* and who secretly spends the early morning hours listening to religious music.

In the folk art and craft scene, Martand Singh, with the support of the cultural czarina Pupul Jayakar and his group of talented gay designers, carved out a place for himself, challenging Rajeev Sethi, the great showman. Martand Singh dominated the Festivals of India and Intach at home and in England.

A number of people vied for the title of the cultural czarina and czar. Ashok Vajpeyi of Bharat Lok Kala Bhavan of Bhopal was one such aspirant. Unfortunately the Bhavan went into decline post Swaminathan. Kapila Vatsyayan of the Indira Gandhi National Centre for Arts, evolved an ambitious programme to rescue the art and culture of India. Unfortunately, Ignca was run as a one woman show with sycophants surrounding her. She did manage to put up some excellent seminars and exhibitions. However, they were not monumental, as the first edition of the Ignca Journal claimed. Mala Singh of *India Magazine*, *Seminar* and Business India TV, too had ambitions, but no funds. She was another minor czarina with her own coterie.

The '80s saw a new cultural czar begin his rise. O.P. Jain, who built his millions from the paper trade had made a tentative entrance into the cultural world in the '60s by supplying paper for Mulk Raj Anand's plush edition of *Kama Sutra*, known best for Mulk's failure to put inverted commas at the beginning and end of the text. Later, with the help of Jyotindra Jain, who came from Ahmedabad to build up a remarkable Crafts Museum from the bureaucratic mess of the handloom and handicrafts organizations, he set up a Museum of Everyday Art in the basement of his Safdarjung Enclave house. His cultural and political contacts helped him expand his empire by acquiring prime land in Mehrauli-Gurgaon. Shared with others, it became the location for Anandgram, a beautifully maintained cultural centre. His Sanskriti Trust, known for recognizing young artists and Anandgram consolidated his presence in the cultural, social and political orbit of Delhi. Today some of the finest functions are organized by O.P. and people vie with one another to be invited.

Lone voices were raised to challenge these Goliaths, like Ram Dhamija, who investigated and wrote about Pupal Jayakar's misdemeanors and the authoritarian attitude of Kapila Vatsyayan in the flimsy magazine, *Arts and Crafts Monthly*. Everyone who read his column encouraged him to continue, for he said what no one else dared to say but would like to. Soon even that magazine was closed by the owner, who came under pressure.

The cultural world now constituted big money because of government, corporate and international patronage. Cut throat competition became the order of the day. The media also became involved, recklessly promoting artists, never mind the talent or involvement in creative expression.

Despite all this, Delhi provided for those of us, who lived our lives far away from the corridors of power, a rich and varied cultural scene. Talented young artists in all fields and some extraordinary minds continue to enrich our lives as we laugh our way into the sunset. Today we curse Delhi, moan about the lack of values and rampant corruption and yet we can never leave the city until our dying day, refusing to believe that even our last rites may be held up because of a power failure.

Literature's Delhi

RANJANA SENGUPTA

DELHI has suffered from having a vivid, romantic history as far as its chroniclers are concerned. The pleasures of its past are so seductive, so full of the fall of empires, courtly intrigues, decadence and romantic decay, that its present appears arid in comparison. While some recent fiction is set in contemporary Delhi, given the rate and scale of high profile book launches in the capital, Delhi life is still relatively uncharted. English fiction writers have not evoked love in the lobby of Anupam PVR, angst in the lanes of West Kidwai Nagar and DLF's Malibu Towne does figure in the pages of an Indo-Anglian bestseller.

If anything, the social mores of present day Delhi are more likely to be found in research oriented commentaries that draw an apocalyptic picture of Delhi's urban chaos. Sadly, contemporary Delhi has few loyalists in literary-academic circles. Recently, for instance, in *Delhi, Urban Space and Human Destinies* (Manohar 2000), a collection of essays on the city's social structure and politics, the editors could boldly assert that 'hardly anyone is ready to declare a passion for Delhi.'

Delhi's apparent lack of a single, territory-wide regional identity has been a disadvantage. There is no *one* real Delhi world that can be evoked with its complement of mythology, ritual and relatives – the literary recipe that is said to appeal to western literary agents in search of the next Arundhati Roy. Yet Delhi's many separate universes are ripe for the plucking (or writing).

Where is the three-generation Delhi kayasth novel, for instance, with its beginnings in a *haveli* in the Chelpuri *mohalla*, a middle section in Civil Lines and a triumphant end in Lodi Estate? If the defining moment of today's Delhi was Partition (and few will disagree), the fictionalized refugee saga, tracking the terrible journey from Lahore to early years in Malviya Nagar, and ending in a farmhouse in Chattarpur, is still unwritten.

And, what about the ultimate Page Three book, a sort of Bridget Jones of Vasant Vihar? This classic is yet unpenned. The emotional life of the city is recorded daily, and in detail, in newspapers and glossy magazines but we still do not have a definitive novel about the inner lives of the fashion frat, for instance. Nor an account of the journey from DDA flats Vasant Kunj to the Miss Universe pageant in the Philippines, a journey Indian beauty contestants make with unfailing regularity.

Frivolous, self-indulgent and irrelevant, the literati will exclaim, but this *is* the nitty-gritty of Delhi life, every bit as nitty-gritty as alienation in a resettlement colony – but no one has written about that either. Somewhere, there are invisible rules governing what should be written, what makes a valid story, what will sell – and writers in Delhi appear to heed such messages unquestioningly. Being in the national capital gives an unnecessary burden of false gravitas to potential writers. The siren calls of recent politics, social inequality and historical trends fetter their imaginations.

It is acceptable in Delhi to explore Page Three – and popular culture generally – through exhibitions or op-ed articles which provide the requisite anthropological distance. But to plunge right in, to immerse yourself unreservedly in that world, is to accept that it is as valid as your own, and this will never do. This will disturb the hierarchies, set in stone, that have governed English-speaking intellectual life in Delhi since well before independence.

This conflict is at its most visible in the media. The realities of circulation and ratings have led to popular culture in the form of showbiz, soaps, songs and gossip getting more and more column space and airtime. The intelligentsia has watched its own previously unbreachable bastions crumble. They have turned to history to political analysis to heritage – anything that will strengthen their position as the sole interpreters and inheritors of this anarchic, untamable city with its untrammelled, extravagant aspirations.

This is why literature in English on Delhi is so weighted in terms of its history, politics and civic chaos. Yet, despite its occasionally narrow reach, it is, almost all of it, unquestioningly secular; there is an acceptance, even admiration, for all ways of life. Thus, the quintessential Delhi novel, where the city has an autonomous role that defines the behaviour of the protagonists, is Ahmed Ali's *Twilight in Delhi* (OUP 1940). It is an elegy to – an even then – vanishing society, an ode to a generation that knew their world was dying. Its power lies in the deliberately nostalgic tone, the note of despair, of gentle, elegant defeat. The city is wonderfully and vividly evoked, its very streets conjuring melancholy:

'This was the street of druggists and *hakims*. With the smell the thought of death came into his mind… he began to think of Babban Jan. Her thought was sad and sweet, like the memory of some dear one dead…'

This vision, this sense of a wistful, irretrievably lost past is so compelling, that in William Dalrymple's *City of Djinns* (Flamingo 1994) which purports to be about a sojourn in the present, is actually all about his search for the past. I have no argument with this, except this winsomely charming book rubbishes the present in order to enhance the gossamer allure of an older, more gracious Delhi.

In this strange competition, the present is represented by Dalrymple's Punjabi landlady and Punjabi taxi driver, who are drawn as venal, shallow and brash. Obdurate customs officials and postmen have walk-on parts. The past is championed by a Persian scholar, a pigeon fancier, an elderly Anglo-Indian lady and other exotic and threatened species. The past, quite naturally, wins hands down.

But the causes of this glamorous, swashbuckling history have been for reasons as mundane as commerce, strategy and geography. 'There is nothing mystical about Delhi as the capital city of India,' writes Percival Spear dampeningly in *Delhi Through the Ages* (ed. R.E. Frykenberg, OUP 1986), a wonderful collection of essays, many of which combine academic rigour with a marvellously vivid, anecdotal style. And, historian Narayani Gupta punctures the myth of the sad-eyed, wilting denizen of the Old City with a telling phrase that has stuck in my mind for years. In the 19th century, the older Delhis were called Khandrat Kalan or the Great Ruins. Here, she writes, 'the people from Shahjahanabad dug perseveringly in the hope of turning up a hoard of coins.' The past, for them, was not just an idea to be wept over, but a source of potential profit.

Another splendid collection is *Historic Delhi* (ed. H.K. Kaul, OUP 1985), an anthology of writing on Delhi over the centuries, both the well-known and the obscure. One of my favourites is Val C. Prinsep, an undazzled witness to the first Delhi Durbar of 1877: 'The size is like a gigantic circus and the decorations are in keeping.' Also illuminating 19th century Shahjahanabad as less than blissful is *The Bride's Mirror* (Permanent Black 2001) by Nazir Ahmad. This is a stern, cautionary tale of two sisters, the saintly (and shrewd) Ashgari, who reforms her gambling husband and manages his appointment to a well-paid post in Sialkot, and the wilful, spoilt Akbari, who gets the fate she deserves when her trousseau is eaten up by white ants.

Closer to our own time, M.M. Kaye's autobiography, *The Golden Afternoon* (Viking 1997), unapologetically outlines the sheer fun of British social life in the Delhi of the '30s. It was a ceaseless whirl between dinners at Akbar Road bungalows, followed by balls at the Viceroy's House and ending with impromptu dances to a wind-up gramophone in the moonlit environs of Humayan's tomb.

Life for the Indians was fortunately less socially exhausting. The late Sheila Dhar gave a vivid account of a Civil Lines childhood in *Here's Someone I'd Like You to Meet* (OUP 1999). Mukul Kesavan's *Looking Through Glass* (Chatto and Windus 1995) visits the India of 1942 and though most of the action is set in Banaras and Lucknow, Delhi is a familiar yet unfamiliar place, the protagonist having travelled back in time from the present. He finds his old school, St. Xavier's, is the Cecil Hotel; his old college, St. Stephen's, in another location.

For time travellers, yearning for the past has its problems: 'A place had changed names and a name had changed places, creating practical difficulties for memory and nostalgia.' (In a neat reversal, James Cameron stayed in the Cecil Hotel in 1946 and records in *Indian Summer* (Penguin 1987) that he went back in the '70s to find his old room was now a classroom crammed with desks.)

While the definitive English novel on Partition is still unwritten, Urvashi Butalia's *The Other Side of Silence* (Viking 1998) puts on record the unheard voices of Partition, 'the smaller, more invisible figures' who endured silently the repercussions of historical forces when they sunder private lives. In another tone altogether, Anita Desai, in *Clear Light of Day* (Heinemann 1980) explores the impact of the traumatic events of 1947 on delicate relationships between siblings living in a decaying old bungalow in north Delhi, which epitomizes their lives. Old Delhi is a metaphor here for wasted lives and unspoken resentments.

'It seemed to her that the dullness and the boredom of her childhood, her youth, were stored here in the room under the worn dusty red rugs, in the bloated brassware, behind the yellowed photographs in the oval frames...'

Much of the literature on Delhi written after independence celebrates the new feel to the city, limping gamely out of the Partition holocaust. The looted Muslim homes, the encampments of refugees, the totally disrupted lives; but there was hope then. Asok Mitra's *Delhi Capital City* (Publications Division 1970) essentially deals with demographic patterns, but while regretting the lost stately graces of the old city in 1947:

'The old enchanting paved courts with the deep stairwells of light, the chiaroscuro of Chowry Bazar, the filtered twilight on the lotus ponds of third floor apartments on G.B. Road...'

Mitra goes on to relate how a young Sikh orphan hawking newspapers, who refused the two *anna* coin Mitra offered, humbled him. 'He did not want my coin unless I wanted his paper.'

The paradoxes of independent India struck James Cameron acutely in Delhi, for which he admits a 'perverse affection'. In *Indian Summer*, Cameron's account is of his visit to India, three decades after his first in the feverish months of 1946 when 'the fading Raj was at grips with its inescapable moment of truth.' Cameron's attitude to Delhi and to India is, like many men of his generation, informed by his view of the first prime minister: 'I think Jawaharlal Nehru was the most important man I ever met...' he states unambiguously. And though he was later alienated by Nehru's inability to stem the corruption and misrule around him during his final years, he nonetheless concludes that Nehru's greatest quality, and one that survived to the end, was that 'he could take the curse out of moral platitudes by believing in them.'

Such charitable assessments are not shared by V.S. Naipaul in *An Area of Darkness* (Andre Deutsch 1964). He is contemptuous of the 'comic little cupolas' of Ashoka Hotel and irritated by the self-importance of the Indian capital in the '60s.

'I could sense its excitement as a new capital city ...a city to which importance had newly come... A city doubly unreal rising suddenly out of the plain – acres of 17th and 18th century ruins, then the ultra-contemporary exhibition buildings.'

Jan Morris takes the other route, the well-trodden one memorialized by E.M. Forster that sees India as a profoundly mysterious, fatalistic, Oriental blur. In 'Mrs. Gupta Never Rang' anthologized in *City Improbable* (ed. Khushwant Singh, Viking 2001), she raises the hoary chestnuts of lazy officials speaking ungrammatical English and never delivering. Delhi, and by extension India, she concludes profoundly, 'is always as it is.'

Delhi's own contemporary chroniclers have often been less than kind, overcome by its ferocious, unstoppable drive toward upward mobility. This drive is expressed in various ways, one of which is architecture. Gautam Bhatia's trenchant comments on Delhi's buildings are well known, but one can sense his nonplussed rage over a cityscape that refuses to listen to reason. In *Punjabi Baroque* (Penguin 1994) he writes,

'But the Punjabi had never been satisfied with his Indian origins anyway... His Panchsheel Park house (was built) in his own image of a country manor, its servant's quarter a plaster replica of Chombord. A Buddhist pagoda roof, when set on a structure of Roman Corinthian columns, was seen by the Punjabi as a structure fit to provide shade to his red Maruti.'

Not everyone reacts with distaste to the brazen, eclectic pastiche of the very, very new. In the beautifully photographed *Delhi's Historic Villages* (Ravi Dayal, 1997), Charles and Karoki Lewis do not unequivocally condemn the transformation of Hauz Khas village into a shopping precinct, which combines Rajput, Mughal, Indo-Saracenic and Moorish elements in a kind of architectural cacophony. Lewis quotes an unnamed visitor as saying: 'The transformation is not entirely unappealing.'

In the glossy, coffee table *Millennium Book on New Delhi* (ed. B.P. Singh and Pavan K. Varma, OUP 2001), Khushwant Singh describes what became of the city after 1947: 'Punjabis imposed their own way of living on the city. Emphasis was on good food and ostentatious display of wealth.' In the same book, Madhu Jain tracks the social trajectory of Delhi in the last 50 years. In *The Happening City*, she writes that the city's intellectual horizon has expanded. Where once the IIC was 'the lone intellectual lodestar for a long while,' today Delhi has changed.

'Status withstood the onslaught of time, fashion and democracy. Then, however, came the brand invasion, and along with it new social ladders to accommodate the rupee and dollar-rich classes... The old crème de la crème with thick silver frames and bejewelled sepia relatives... now sup with the corporate world.'

The change in Delhi's social vocabulary is examined by Pavan K. Varma in *The Great Indian Middle Class* (Penguin 1998). The post liberalization scenario had a profound impact on the middle class mindset. 'The removal of any stigma associated with making money has ended hypocrisy but also the need to be concerned about anything else.' In a memorable passage, Varma describes a 'loo' theme party held at a farmhouse where the guests came dressed in bathroom apparel.

'Is this grand party idea just a frivolous, juvenile ripple of the affluent class? Or is there just the hint of the vulgar and the perverse? Not in moral terms ...but in what the evening demonstrates: the unthinking acceptance of the enormous gulf that separates a tiny group of people living out, bang in the middle of a semi-rural setting, an idiom that fits in with the wild side of Manhattan... from thousands of people just yards away who walk a kilometre or more to obtain something as basic as drinking water.'

Fictional portraits of contemporary Delhi are thin on the ground. Delhi's greatest living chronicler, Khushwant Singh's column, 'With Malice Toward One and All' in *The Hindustan Times*, has for decades monitored the whims and ripples of this extraordinary city. His monumental novel, *Delhi* (Penguin 2000), has traced the checkered, romantic and terrible history of this city with characteristic rumbustiousness.

But there is no recent portrait of the machinations of the political class, the brittle angst of the haute bourgeois or the new ariviste post Partition class that is soaring upwards on the wings of fashion, media or politics. Nayantara Sahgal once chronicled the doings of such people, and *Rich Like Us* (Heinemann 1985) tackles the themes of the Emergency, affluent socialists and unhappy civil servants.

The same world was also the stamping ground of Ruth Prawer Jhabvala, before she moved out of it, but a fairly recent collection of stories reprises the same milieu. In *East into Upper East* (John Murray 1998), 'Development and Progress', for instance, is set in the '60s and exemplifies Jhabvala's mix of fascination and distaste for a particular kind of Indian. The story concerns a young British diplomat, Kitty, who falls under the spell of a brother and two sisters who live in a mansion in Civil Lines. The brother, an IAS officer, is full of the Nehruvian rhetoric of the time and Kitty is much taken with him and with the big, rambling house filled with friends, relatives and servants. Then fast-forward 30 years: one of the sisters has committed suicide, the other is bitter and lonely and the brother is a mixture of pomposity and frustration.

Sagarika Ghose's *The Gin Drinkers* (HarperCollins 2000) taps into a younger, newer Delhi. An Oxbridge educated generation, with idealism and ambition in unequal proportions, grapple with the issues of social deprivation, relationships which founder on accusations of intellectual or ideological dishonesty and parents who are strangers. Coming home after several years at university, the protagonist Uma noted,

'The roundabouts surrounding Rajpath still looked the same. But just a few minutes walk away, in Connaught Place the rubble of new construction loomed through a permanent haze of dust. In the government colonies, white or yellow-washed bungalows with their bougainvillea garlands teetered on the edge of clamorous flyovers. Delhi was changing muddily.'

The world that Anjana Appachana evokes in *Listening Now* (IndiaInk 1998) is uncharted; it's the quiet world of middle class colonies, of the ceaseless irritation of complaining mothers-in-law and silent, non-communicative husbands. It tells you how within this world, dismissed as humdrum and ordinary, there is hope, anticipation and wild tragedy; she gives dignity to the mundane. Delhi as it was in the '70s seeps out all over this book and that is part of its appeal for me: it was Delhi before Barista, before Archies, before growing up.

Appachana evokes the afternoons in the British Council Library when it was in the Aifacs building, the slow DTC buses, the bookshops in Connaught Place and the college conversations about who had 'topped their year.' Susan Visvanathan's *The Visiting Moon* (IndiaInk 2002) summons up the world of Patparganj housing societies, the muddy vegetable markets, the anonymity of identical flats, the ferocity of intellectual argument among the young professionals that people the area – the whole way of life that has evolved across the river.

Delhi has thus been immortalized in many *avatars* and I have omitted for lack of space, the accounts of its political history – the Emergency, the 1984 riots and the recorded musings of its leaders. But despite this vast quantity and usually high quality of writing on Delhi, the terrain is still patchily illuminated. There are still huge swathes of darkness where brave explorers need to go.